"It's been said that the glory of _____ that statement perfectly captures Ab_____ *Celibate Sex*. She may have written this _____ singles, but she's invited every human soul into the journey of a lifetime—the journey of awakening to the relentless grace and pursuit of a Savior."

—MIKE FOSTER, executive director and cofounder, People of the Second Chance

"Too often the church has avoided addressing issues concerning sexuality and singleness, not because they are unimportant but because people don't want to get dirty in the process. Allow Abbie Smith to take you into these topics through her honest exploration of her own journey. Allow her to put voice to the questions plaguing many in the church today."

—KYLE STROBEL, assistant professor of theology, Grand Canyon University; author of *Formed for the Glory of God*

"*Celibate Sex* takes complex and difficult subject matter and invites honest, helpful discussion and thought. Abbie addresses such topics as sex, sexuality, and identity within the biblical context in a mature and relatable way. Her fresh voice, candid questions, and desire to lead people into an honest dialogue are refreshing and challenging. My hope is that this book would open conversations and stir your heart to become more of who God has uniquely created you to be."

—JEANNE STEVENS, lead pastor, Soul City Church, Chicago

"*Celibate Sex* is an honest look at singleness, sexuality, and God's love for humanity. Abbie Smith shares her heart and is unafraid to tackle tough questions with honesty and a raw transparency that will resonate with this generation of young, single Christ followers."

—BRIAN ROTTSCHAFER, college life groups associate pastor, Rock Harbor Church, Costa Mesa, California

"*Celibate Sex* is a breath of fresh air that offers an authentic and biblical perspective about life, struggles, and sexuality. I encourage you to let Abbie Smith lead you on this journey to unpack truths that will change the course of your life."

—JORDAN TERRELL, college pastor at Flatirons Community Church, Lafayette, Colorado

"A wildly courageous exploration of single spirituality. This woman loves God and the Bible. She will make you think and teach you how to think. I wouldn't have come to some of the same conclusions she has, but then I've never thought about this topic as deeply, suffered as much, or wondered as thoughtfully as she has on behalf of millions of Christians. I defer to her wisdom."

—JIM HENDERSON, founder, jimhendersonpresents.com

"I am excited about Abbie Smith's work. Her insights are fresh yet wise. I am confident her book will help singles work their way through the labyrinth of confusion and the cacophonous voices of the media distracting them from wholeness and peace."

—JERRY ROOT, PhD, associate professor, Wheaton College

"Having worked with hundreds of college students and twentysomethings and having experienced their dissatisfaction with cliché answers regarding this topic, I appreciate the way Abbie Smith has pushed this discussion to a deeper level. She moves toward the heart of the issues of our sexuality and helps people see that God is there waiting for us with true freedom within which He has created us to live."

—MATT METZGER, college pastor and site pastor, Blackhawk Church Downtown, Madison, Wisconsin

ABBIE SMITH

CELIBATE *SEX*

Musings on Being

Loved,

Single,

Twisted,

and Holy

NAVPRESS
Discipleship Inside Out®

NAVPRESS

Discipleship Inside Out®

NavPress is the publishing ministry of The Navigators, an international Christian organization and leader in personal spiritual development. NavPress is committed to helping people grow spiritually and enjoy lives of meaning and hope through personal and group resources that are biblically rooted, culturally relevant, and highly practical.

For a free catalog go to www.NavPress.com or call 1.800.366.7788 in the United States or 1.800.839.4769 in Canada.

ISBN-13: 978-1-61291-353-7

Library of Congress Cataloging-in-Publication Data has been requested.

Printed in the United States of America

1 2 3 4 5 6 7 8 / 18 17 16 15 14 13

CONTENTS

INTRODUCTION

What if being a disciple is an authentic response to being loved? And what if being loved actually feels like being loved? Not like some abstract belief we adhere to, not like something so-called-purely-spiritual, as if there could be such a thing, but something that has to do with the part of us that thirsts and hungers and feels and suffers and loves and cries, our passions, our needs, what is thoroughly and essentially human in us. . . . God's love is that connected to what we need, to our guts, to our passion, to our essential humanness.

DEBBIE BLUE, *Sensual Orthodoxy*

I DIDN'T GROW up knowing God, but I grew up knowing what God thought, such as "Sex before marriage is bad." I heard it in a Sunday school class I visited in elementary school. I was confused, though, because surely having babies was good, but didn't having babies happen from sex? Further perplexing was the TV series I saw in sixth grade, where a young girl had an abortion for fear of being disowned by her religious family. Then at my Catholic high school's homecoming dance, I heard that slow dancing should "leave room for the Holy Spirit," and then from a guy in college that "I couldn't know God if I hadn't had sex." So by the age of eighteen, I was utterly confused about God, sex, and God's thoughts about sex.

My freshman year of college found me searching for something other than this world's offerings. I had everything the world could offer, it seemed: a family who loved me, friends who liked me, and the front doorstep of the college of my dreams. Yet something deep within remained markedly empty—and tired. Tired of working for love and performing in hopes of being liked. Tired of searching for belonging and reaching for a next rung.

I took a world religions class my first semester, studying multiple faiths and faith practices. Nothing struck me quite as compellingly as grace, as told by the story of Christianity. According to my studies, a man named Jesus could see my brokenness and offered His own life to heal it. Furthermore, He was said to seek me, love me, and save me before I could muster up the energy toward any such attempt. Plus, still confused by elementary impressions of sex and Holy Spirit stuff, I at least wanted to gain some grasp of what was true.

About this time, I developed my first "Christian crush." The guy invited me to a campus ministry, which seemed odd as a first attempt at hitting on me, but I tagged along anyway. The raised hands and swaying arms were a bit much, but the people seemed all right, so I decided to stay—and return the next week, and the week after. Though my crush began to fizzle with the falling leaves, attendance at churchy events didn't. I liked being with these Jesus people and observing how and why they ticked. It was fascinating and alluring and couldn't help but wear off on me. So through a slow, jagged process—unexpected though it was, given my background and upbringing—I yielded into relationship with Jesus that year.

Involvement with the church scene and its churchy people became a new way of life for me. I learned about prayer and the gospel and telling God the desires of my heart. And for the most part, He seemed faithful. But there was one area that I couldn't seem to articulate clearly enough or that God couldn't seem to understand: I wanted to get married. And as a maturing Christian woman, I thought I was *supposed* to get married. But God didn't hear me, I guess. Or He did hear me but chose to ignore me. Either way, He didn't give me a husband. And I didn't know what to do about it. Nor did I know what to do with the hormones and horrible hours of loneliness that accompanied my solo plight.

My midtwenties found me even more alone and confused. I wasn't just confused about sex anymore, and God's views on sex; I was confused about marriage as well—and prayer, desires, my body, dreams, and unmet longings too. I thought I'd done what a good Christian should do, yet I remained single and unsure of just about everything. Could I even be a mature godly woman and not be married? Was it possible to be whole and holy apart from holy matrimony? *I should be married by now*, I thought, *with baby number two on the way. Or if not married, at least making some grandiose movement toward world peace or saving Darfur.* But I wasn't: I was single, and I felt singled out by longing, sexual and otherwise.

The world told me to give up my strict standards and romanticized rules of chastity; the church told me to pray harder and cling tighter to them. And both sides would say unhelpful things like, "Just stop looking, honey, and Mr. Right will come around the corner," "Start being more content with yourself," "Stick to these rules," "Serve more," and "I wonder what you're doing wrong." So was my singleness my fault, then? And would getting married somehow make everything right, like my sexuality and misfit roles? And God—well, I wasn't sure what to think about God anymore. Did He really care if I was married or not? Did He really want to give me the desires of my heart? And if so, what was I doing wrong to prevent such an offering? It felt as if I were failing God by not being who or where I was supposed to be by this point. What "fruitful offspring" could I boast of—a degree, a job, my own apartment? If I died tomorrow, what would people say at my funeral? What had I produced or offered by my existence? Had my life left any imprint on this side of heaven? Nope. Nada. Nothing. Or at least that's how I felt. I didn't fit into society, and I certainly didn't fit into formats of the modern church.

Singles today are widows of sorts (see Acts 6:1-8), needing to be listened to and needing a framework for who we are and how we fit into the Christian family.[1] What does it mean to abstain from sex while respecting sexual wirings? What does it mean to be content in one's singleness while longing toward marriage? Can I be sexual without a spouse? And is a spouse something I'm allowed to keep hoping for? What does it mean to be beautiful and embody sexuality? What does it mean to wait well and proactively and to desire genuinely and passionately?

These pages will dive head-on into all of the above—into the muddy devotions of a modern single—possibly to start shaping a foundation of single theology that's been quiet in the church for far too long. For singles especially, the space between dismissing one's sexuality altogether, as if it's too holy, and letting it drive us, as if it's our sole identity, is vast in measure and crucial to explore. We are made in God's image, and He's allowing us to explore that image and how it relates to sex and love and the church and our roles therein (see Psalm 139:1). But will we allow ourselves? (Note "For Further Musing and Discussion" found at the end of each chapter. This section is meant to move us toward such allowance. And feel free to move beyond and between and into the margins of these questions. They are but a guide.)

There seem to be two kinds of people: those who have questions and ask them, and those who have questions. I prefer to be the kind who asks. I think it's a human thing to have questions but a humility thing to find courage enough to put them into question. Asking means admitting that I don't have all the answers. It means that I need you—that *I* is dependent on *we*. In my singleness, sexuality, humanity, emotionality, physicality, and—I suppose most of all—spirituality, I need you. And in some way or another, you need me. And we both need Jesus.

We were not made to be alone, yet too often this remains the predicament for we who remain unhitched. That's what this book is about. It's about being hitched and not being hitched; it's about community and sexuality, longings and learning to follow Jesus. It's about understanding ourselves, as created in the image of God, *even* (and maybe *especially*) in our sexuality. It's about finding home, in our bodies and in our humanity, in our brokenness and in God's divinity. It's about becoming human and finding Love.

FOR FURTHER MUSING AND DISCUSSION

1. How do you relate to these pages? Did anything strike you as surprising? Familiar?
2. What are you interested in, or confused about, regarding God and sexuality? What are you hoping to learn or better understand about yourself from reading this book?

He's not safe, but he's good.

C. S. LEWIS

CHAPTER 1

FIG LEAVES

Nothing is more practical than finding God; that is, falling in love in a quite absolute, final way. What you are in love with, what seizes your imagination, will affect everything. It will decide what will get you out of bed in the morning, what you will do with your evenings, how you will spend your weekends, what you read, who you know, what breaks your heart, and what amazes you with joy and gratitude. Fall in love; stay in love, and it will decide everything.

PEDRO ARRUPE, S. J.

FOR ME, THE journey of sexuality started with a kiss — a delectable, luscious, seductive kiss. You might've called it ambiguous, but I would've called it as penetrating and lucid as a dive into cold water. It aroused my senses and awakened my taste buds. It was everything I'd ever dreamed of, and it made me want more. The problem was the magazine article I'd read just hours before. It radiated off the rack, telling me kisses were erotic and even a potential aphrodisiac, which was more than troubling for my God-following brain. I decided I had two options: I could curse Hershey for the rest of my life, or I could explore the possibility of tasting good chocolate while attempting to taste and see, too, that *the Lord is good* (see Psalm 34:8).

That same evening, I received an uncanny phone call from my pregnant sister. Her rapid breathing alarmed me, but I quickly realized that Courtney was breathtaken not out of fear but out of awe. She was standing with a crowd of more than one hundred worshipful women at

Boston's *Sex and the City* premiere, hearing a soundtrack of high-pitched squeals and flabbergasted descriptions of Carrie Bradshaw costumes.

Sex sells in our culture and holds little prejudice, or restriction, in its pursuit. What, though, does this mean for the *abstinent* one? What does it mean for the single, chased by the same orgasmic ends even while committed to desires of remaining chaste? Can I be sexual and pure in the same sentence? Can my singleness share a bed with both chastity and freedom? Can God entertain my requests for things repressed and revealed, things sensual and real? These questions are too often left ignored, especially in the church.

Not being hitched doesn't gel with the late-twenties schema. And I certainly didn't plan, or want, to be the one to write this book, because I didn't plan, or want, to be the one who was single in her late twenties. Nor did I want to be coined as "the girl who writes about singles." I thought I'd get married at twenty-four. I got my driver's license at sixteen and legitimate ID at twenty-one, so why shouldn't marriage have a marked, predictable age too?

About midway through my twenty-third year, however, I started doubting my prophecies. A few years later, I *really* doubted them. And somewhere in the latter part of my third decade, I had a maybe obvious, but definitely overlooked, realization that I am single today and, more than that, that it's possible I'll be single tomorrow and every tomorrow thereafter. No one had ever dangled that (rotten) carrot in front of me. Instead, they said things like, "You must be trying too hard" or "You must not be trying hard enough. Put yourself out there more, Abbie—date, do eHarmony." Essentially, every pulpit, person, and magazine in the grocery store checkout line had its unique explanation as to why I wasn't married. Never had it occurred to me, then, that singleness might *not* simply be based on something I did or didn't do (bad dater, bad kisser, too pushy, too many issues, too needy, not needy enough, too skinny, too fat, too bald, too poor, too rich, too controlling, not controlling enough). And, in fact, maybe my "not married" status had a precise, thought-out meaning behind it.

In grade school, I was the one who got squeamish at most words in sex-ed class, so I certainly didn't expect to be writing a book about sexuality in my twenties. Furthermore, anatomical names are called "privates" for a reason, I thought, and anything in their sphere seemed "wrong" to me, certainly when mentioned alongside "Jesus." Thus, I was back at the Hershey dilemma. Either I could curse God and stumble ahead in my confused single life, or I could request His help in learning to taste and see life and pleasure and singleness in another way. Did He have a liturgy capable of handling my complexities? And what would it look like to "unprivatize" topics such as sex and sexual addiction, not in order to be ultraliberal, but to become authentic?

I'm not a bra-burning feminist[1] or bitter at men for acting like boys or at women for trying to lead like men. And I'm not out to blame. I'm just a normal gal who's hit some realizations that never marked her radar screen, though it seems as if they should have. So I decided to put some thoughts to paper. Solving all quandaries of singleness isn't my goal, nor is pronouncing you bound for hell because you're sleeping with your boyfriend. I simply want to ponder some thoughts on being home, in love, and sexual, *in Christ*. In the words of Henri Nouwen, "Demons love darkness and hiddenness. Inner fears and struggles which remain isolated develop great power over us. But when we talk about them in a spirit of trust, then they can be looked at and dealt with. Once brought into the light of mutual love, demons lose their power and quickly leave us."[2]

Things make more sense when you know the whole story. Mystery novels aren't mysterious once you know who the killer is or puzzles puzzling when you know where all the pieces belong. It's the in-between that's perplexing. And herein lies me: I have an addictive focus on greener grass and sunnier skies, feeling stuck in a span of cloudy beginnings and unfinished (or obsolete altogether) ends, questioning what's true and what I thought would be true about this point in my life. I expected certain ends, which have somehow only landed me back at blank beginnings. It's like time is two-faced: It claims to be on my side but also screams opposing captions and mockingly dangles carrots of being both for me and against me.

My daydreams, night dreams, talking, and prayer are a lot more about where I'm going than where I am. And I'm starting to realize that the more I live *there*, the less capacity I have for *here*; the more I lust after who I am *not*, the less security I have for who I *am*. Such lusting didn't start out tainted, though. It was created *good*; it wasn't until the logic of a serpent[3] became more mesmerizing than the logic of God that the likes of lust, love, and purity became tainted thereafter (see Genesis 2–3). This fall of man hijacked God's original design, and we humans have been wearing fig leaves ever since. Once naked and unashamed, we're now in a perpetual fight against shame, aware of our perversions and awakened by cravings for coverage and the safety of a mask.

Masks mask us, and that can be good. But masks hide us, and that can be bad, preventing us from ever truly seeing ourselves. We never see the Truth. Masks keep us convinced that who we are is too much or not enough and that God's pursuits of restoration are insufficient. Masks convince us that we're safe only behind a lie.

The fig leaves (see Genesis 3:7) we wear may change throughout the ages, but we all wear masks and have a multitude of options lining our closets. A contemporary menu may include busyness, isolation, noise, notoriety, porn, perfectionism, perfected theology, asceticism, athleticism, sarcasm, self-comfort, self-help, self-loathing, being hip, Facebook, food addiction, false securities, exercise addiction, false stories, false idols, fake identities, fake interests, fake lovers, fake boobs, fantasies, Web surfing, soul searching, stock markets, subcultures, culture, cults, religion, reason, intellect, and the list goes on. Some obviously look stronger, sexier, or more significant than others, and not all masks are bad in and of themselves. All masks have the potential to hide us, though, and to help aid us in our proclivity toward covering and coping.

Eventually, masks illegitimately sleep with my longings, and stuff gets ugly and destructive—fast. Masks suppress my longings, and suppressing requires that I breed secrets (in order to cope with what I know as the truth). Secrets breed shame; shame breeds silence; silence breeds silenced hopes; silenced hopes breed sequential letdowns; sequential letdowns breed exponential shame. And the cycle goes on.

That's the paralyzing, depressing side of the story. But here's the good news: God knew of humankind's fall before we fell. He knew that forms of hiding would always be readily available. He knew every brand of coping and how it would fit into every human being's wardrobe, dressing our nakedness and concealing our shame. And He made a Way out.

FOR FURTHER MUSING AND DISCUSSION

1. What does this quote mean to you?

> Sex sells in our culture and holds little prejudice, or restriction, in its pursuit. What, though, does this mean for the *abstinent* one? What does it mean for the single, chased by the same orgasmic ends even while committed to desires of remaining chaste? Can I be sexual and pure in the same sentence? Can my singleness share a bed with both chastity and freedom? Can God entertain my requests for things repressed and revealed, things sensual and real? These questions are too often left ignored, especially in the church.

2. The last four paragraphs of this chapter address masks. What masks do you see in our culture? In the church? In yourself? What do you think keeps us running back to our masks?

Hope

The reason I hate hope is because it leaves me hoping.

It answers vaguely enough to hold my attention, but varied enough to further my lusts, which if left deferred, grow my heart sick.

Hope pursues me relentlessly, and invites me anew. It asks me to go deeper, and tells me deeper is where I'll be found.

I concede, only because I hope such telling is true.

CHAPTER 2

SEX AND UNION

The "outward" interpretation of spiritual formation, emphasizing specific acts as it does, will merely increase "the 'righteousness' of the scribe and Pharisee." It will not, as we must, "go beyond it" (Matthew 5:20, PAR) to achieve genuine transformation of who I am through and through — Christ's man or woman, living richly in his kingdom.

DALLAS WILLARD, *Renovation of the Heart*

Listen to me, you who pursue righteousness, you who seek the LORD: look to the rock from which you were hewn, and to the quarry from which you were dug.

ISAIAH 51:1

HUMAN SEXUALITY IS at the center of some of today's most heated debates in society and in the church. There are arguments about homosexuality, marriage, roles of men and women, sexual (im)morality, identity, and the list goes on. And underlying each of these debates are core questions of what it means to be human *and* sexual and how our lives as sexual humans should therefore operate. Thus, any meaningful approach to these conversations must begin by looking at sexuality and its relationship to being human. Who we are as human persons is intimately connected to, and inseparable from, who we are as sexual beings. Furthermore, it's impossible to understand the human person apart from understanding God's view of the human person and how God's own life, as revealed in Jesus', orients and grounds understandings of our selves and, thus, our sexuality.

Sex is generally used in reference to the biological drive for union with a person of the opposite sex; *sexuality* references an exploration of what it means to be a man or a woman, or *not* to be a man or *not* to be a woman, including treatments and responses to each other herein. And while sexuality certainly demands considerations of that which is concretely physical, its contents reach far beyond just sex. Sexual expression is about more than simply *doing it* or *not doing it*. Males typically equate "sexuality" and "being sexual" with intercourse, while women tend to think of it in terms of the emotional, physical, and spiritual. For both, though, sexuality arouses deeply embedded aspects of us and often awakens caverns of shame, fear, and unforgiveness.

According to Paul K. Jewett in *Man as Male and Female*,

> Sexuality permeates one's individual being to its very depth; it conditions every facet of one's life as a person. As the self is always aware of itself as an "I," so this "I" is always aware of itself as himself or herself. Our self-knowledge, then, is indelibly bound up not simply with our human being but with our sexual being. At the human level there is no "I" and "thou" per se, but only the "I" who is male or female confronting the "thou," the "other," who is also male or female. The glory of my sexuality is that it knows no limits and oozes easily across lines of "secular" and "sacred" and obliterates anything thought to exist in the realm of "casual."[1]

In the words of Eugene Peterson, "We are sexual beings deeply, thoroughly, and inescapably. In the experience of our sexuality we know another, and, indirectly, ourselves. It is also in our sexuality that we know, or don't know, God."[2]

As I've begun taking God more seriously these past years, I've become captivated by how He sees and creates the world, sustains and redeems the creation. And I've wanted more. I've wanted wider expanses of understanding Him—wider screens of seeing who He really is and what it is He lives for. And I've wanted help understanding me: Who am I and what am I meant to live for? How do my singleness and sexuality fit into my relationship with God, and how does God's existence, as revealed in the life of Jesus, affect mine?

Saint Irenaeus said, "The glory of God is a human being fully alive." How, though, do we find ourselves here? How do we live alive? Or maybe the harder question is, how is it that so many of us spend most of our lives apart from actual living? I think directly and indirectly, a lot has to do with misconstrued and misplaced frameworks of marriage, singleness, sexuality, and our identity in God.

If I'm to stand on the premise that my sexuality is rooted in the image of God, understanding it must begin with God and His revealed image. To embrace my sexuality is to embrace God's design of me, and to engage with God in my sexuality is to engage with my femininity (or masculinity). It is to engage with my distinct nature as a woman: when dancing, when wearing an outfit that makes me feel a certain way, when taking a bath, when being treated respectfully by a guy, or when enjoying music, holding a baby, or sharing a room with friends.

All of our relationships involve sexuality because all of our relationships involve two sexual beings. Am I saying that interactions with your platonic friend, neighbor, boss, or mom have sexual aspects, then? Yes. Our human sexuality expresses itself in every aspect of how we relate to one another as self, man, woman, child, and adult. We bond via sexuality—through moving toward relationship with "the other," as Stanley Grenz refers to it.[3] And in doing so, we expose our drive toward the created order, a first step in establishing our drive toward the broader human community.

Being male or being female has always been a most prominent aspect of our personality and expression, as has our mysterious dependence on each other. From the beginning, man has never been complete without the company of woman, or woman without the company of man. Just as God cannot be understood apart from His own relational existence—eternal Father, infinitely loving His eternal Son, bound up in the unity and communion of the Holy Spirit—so humanity cannot be understood apart from the relationship of the sexes.

Both singleness and marriage, then, should captivate relationship and dependence, not isolation and independence. Understanding sexuality begins with understanding relationship as it is known in the Trinity, the three-in-one Godhead who is mutually indwelling and relationally interpenetrating. All of creation's relationships are positioned to mimic those of the divine, repeating interactions of and between the Father, the Son, and the Holy Spirit. Consider Jesus' prayer in John 17:11-26:

I am no longer in the world, but they are in the world, and I am coming to you. Holy Father, keep them in your name, which you have given me, *that they may be one, even as we are one*. While I was with them, I kept them in your name, which you have given me. I have guarded them, and not one of them has been lost except the son of destruction, that the Scripture might be fulfilled. But now I am coming to you, and these things I speak in the world, *that they may have my joy fulfilled in themselves.* I have given them your word, and the world has hated them because they are not of the world, just as I am not of the world. I do not ask that you take them out of the world, but that you keep them from the evil one. They are not of the world, just as I am not of the world. Sanctify them in the truth; your word is truth. As you sent me into the world, so I have sent them into the world. *And for their sake I consecrate myself, that they also may be sanctified in truth.*

I do not ask for these only, but also for those who will believe in me through their word, *that they may all be one, just as you, Father, are in me, and I in you, that they also may be in us*, so that the world may believe that you have sent me. *The glory that you have given me I have given to them, that they may be one even as we are one, I in them and you in me, that they may become perfectly one, so that the world may know that you sent me and loved them even as you loved me.* Father, I desire that they also, whom you have given me, may be with me where I am, to see my glory that you have given me because you loved me before the foundation of the world. O righteous Father, even though the world does not know you, I know you, and these know that you have sent me. I made known to them your name, and I will continue to make it known, *that the love with which you have loved me may be in them, and I in them.* (emphasis added)

Quintessential spiritual living in the Christian context means that all of me is organized around God as well as sustained and restored by Him. My individuality is based on me as I really am in relation to God. Jesus, therefore, in His union with God and His disciples, models the purest of sexuality, chastity, and relational intimacy. He is called to be one as He and the Father are one, and He prays the same for us. In the life of God, we find three persons upholding one another in love. And while I don't think the triune life was meant as an exact relational blueprint for humankind, I do think Jesus and the triune relationship (between Father, Son, and Holy Spirit) provide us with the fullest image of human relationship and, therefore, our sexuality.

Apart from God, my relationship to you will inevitably turn selfward. In the words of Dietrich Bonhoeffer, "Whereas the primal relationship of man to man is a giving one, in the state of sin it is purely demanding. Every man exists in a state of complete voluntary isolation; each man lives his own life, instead of all living the same God-life."[4] But as Christ followers, we've been given an alternative existence, upholding others as other human beings made in the image of God. We have been invited not to defeat or undermine their identity but to engage with them on a level of real, abundant, everlasting life. Among other things, this is true chastity and nonpossessive sexuality. This is true love: upholding another as another person, not as a way to fulfill my self and desires but as a way to give of myself for another. And in the most mysterious of ways, this giving away of and losing myself is, in fact, the very means to finding my self and to living alive (see Matthew 10:39; 16:25; Mark 8:35; Luke 9:24; 17:33; John 12:25).

The early chapters of the Judeo-Christian Scriptures explain that there is a God who created Adam and Eve, a heterosexual, two-party couple, meant to further create, enjoy, and rule over the earth. The so-called fall of man, however, caused the falling of all things. And all pursuits since have been twisted, to some degree, bereft of Love's original intentions. That's the bad news. The hopeful news is that *humans* fell, not God. Love never changed; humankind's reception of it did. Even in our twisted pursuits, Love kept pursuing, as originally intended.

I heard a lecture recently on sex and sexuality, and the sound bite that stuck was, "The healed state of homosexuality is not heterosexuality but holiness." The sticking for me wasn't as much about being gay or straight as it was about healing. And if the statement is true, which I believe it is, any stray from what it was before the Fall—whether sexual, emotional, psychological, physical—finds healing in a new identity, called "holy."[5]

Faith in Jesus Christ saves us from eternal separation from God and invites us into eternal communion with God. But we're not in heaven yet. There remains a gap between our present earthly state, or *now*, and *then*, when perfection will be fully known. And it is impossible to modify such capacities in and of ourselves. We have unceasing need for God. We cannot *make* Him give us contentment in our sexuality or personality or body image; we cannot make Him give us a boyfriend or spouse or life vocation. But we can ask Him to help us discover His story and our story and to discover contentment resounding in both. Between twisted aspects of where we are and divine aspirations of where we want to be, we find space to become more human and sought by a Savior.

FOR FURTHER MUSING AND DISCUSSION

1. If you are a human being, you are a sexual being. Often, though, we hide or hate this part of us, walking around as partial beings, wondering where we've gone wrong. More times than not, we've failed to develop a healthy construct of what it means to be sexual *and* to be a Christian, meaning we're not experiencing life in its fullness. How does your experience relate to this?

2. This chapter revolves around the following sentences:

   Who we are as human persons is intimately connected to, and insepa-rable from, who we are as sexual beings. Furthermore, it's impossible to understand the human person apart from understanding God's view of the human person and how God's own life, as revealed in Jesus', orients and grounds understandings of our selves and, thus, our sexuality.

   What do you find challenging about these sentences? Do you agree or disagree? Have you seen the church address this well?

3. Spend some time reflecting on this sentence: "Between twisted aspects of where we are and divine aspirations of where we want to be, we find space to become more human and sought by a Savior." What are some twisted aspects of your life and heart today? How does the gospel of Jesus speak into this?

4. Consider Jesus' prayer in John 17. What stands out to you? What do you notice about the relationships between the Father, Son, and Holy Spirit? How might the words of John 17 take residence in your life this week?

To love at all is to be vulnerable. Love anything, and your heart will certainly be wrung and possibly be broken. If you want to make sure of keeping it intact, you must give your heart to no one, not even to an animal. Wrap it carefully round with hobbies and little luxuries; avoid all entanglements; lock it up safe in the casket or coffin of your selfishness. But in that casket — safe, dark, motionless, airless — it will change. It will not be broken; it will become unbreakable, impenetrable, irredeemable. The alternative to tragedy, or at least to the risk of tragedy, is damnation. The only place outside of Heaven where you can be perfectly safe from all the dangers and perturbations of love is Hell.

C. S. LEWIS, *The Four Loves*

CHAPTER 3

ALONE

It is clear that the very first community is that between man and woman. They are one family, one body. If their differences cannot be loved and respected by each other, then unity breaks down; they become rivals and are no longer members of the same body.

JEAN VANIER, *Community and Growth*

WHILE I WAS counseling a single gal recently, we brainstormed about what she could do this particular evening to practice enjoying God's presence. I nonchalantly suggested a walk on the beach.

"That'd be nice, but the thought of people seeing me out there is too much to bear."

"What do you mean? Because you'd start skipping or something . . . or singing 'Jesus Loves Me'?"

"No," she said, chuckling. "Just being by myself. I'm not good at that, and I'm especially not good at letting people see me like that."

"What about going to a movie, and then by the time it's done, it'll be dark outside?"

"Yeah, but same thing. What would I do if someone saw me at the movies . . . *by myself!?*"

We are petrified of being alone. We avoid solo situations and resist aloneness at all costs, even reconvening with exes or returning to abusers because at least being with someone feels better than being alone. When asked in an interview if she was scared of death, well-known French singer Edith Piaf answered, "Not as afraid as I am of solitude."[1]

C. S. Lewis called pain "God's megaphone to rouse a deaf world," but rarely do we treat it that way. Loneliness and aloneness pass us every day but are seldom considered more than a plight. But what if pain were an invitation to worship just as much as (or sometimes more than) joy? What if genuine lament could, in fact, birth liberation? Pain, loneliness, longing, aloneness—what if each of these presented an invitation to access different areas of our souls? What if they were bridges to who we're becoming? In our tears and loneliness, lacking and longing, hurting and aloneness, what if God yearns to be near?

While flying home from a wedding recently, I let God have it. I told Him I couldn't do this anymore. *I'm tired of being single. This is lame. You're lame. I hate singleness.* As I thought these words, my frustrations became greater. But somewhere between the 10,000-feet announcement and landing, I had a weird realization that I wasn't alone in my frustrations. It was Jesus, I remembered, who attended at least a few weddings, so of all people, He must be familiar with standing alone in a crowd of supposed togetherness.

Then I began wondering if Jesus ever felt like I do. Was He confronted with the loneliness of being single? Did He ever feel abandoned? Did Jesus ever feel alone? According to what we're told in the Scriptures, our most plausible answer is yes. And our most plausible explanation, maybe, is that aloneness has the potential to be a gift. It has the capacity to lead us into solitude, or aloneness that transcends loneliness. Entering the practice of solitude, or the presence of aloneness, doesn't promise answers or safeguard our horizons. But it invites us into the glory of true communion and into communion with true glory.

In solitude, we are found *as we are*—you as you, standing face-to-face with yourself, with nowhere to escape. We can lessen solitude's weight or distract its weighty implications, but once felt, something about the raw reality of our true selves will always remain.

If we desire comfort and ease and the romantic highs of an illusion, we should avoid being truly alone at all costs. But if we desire the truth of our selves and the honest state of our souls, we must wholly embrace who we are and who we are not; we must seek solitude and wait for holy union.

We may never find a precise answer for our inner complexities or a relationship that satisfies the endurance of our souls. That is heaven. And that is the fulfillment of the union we were ultimately made for. But the pursuit of this union—and the promise of God to draw near to us along the way (see Psalm 145:18; James 4:8)—remains our deepest and nearest and most powerful hope.

Though awakened in solitude, we are also wired for connection and completion in and through an *other*. That is, we are fundamentally incomplete in and of ourselves. And this wiring is a core aspect of our sexuality and a key bridge to accessing our true humanity. We share an innate longing for relationship and completeness through a community that transcends ourselves. Humans are relational beings, made in God's image. We survive in the context of each other, heal in the community of one another, and will literally die in attempting to do life alone.

Not long ago, I moved across the country. One morning I was struck by the perks that come from being in a new city and not knowing folks, such as waking to an agenda-less Saturday. Whether I made it to the farmers' market or to a dusty aisle of the used-book store was not important. As I departed from my front door, instead of having a prescribed destination in mind, I was determined to let twenty bucks and the wind be my compass.

A park called Forsyth is a stone's throw from my Savannah apartment and shares its south side with an eclectic coffee shop and ever-lively scene. I strolled that way and enjoyed a cookie, a cup of tea, and a scan of the *New York Times* before returning to the park. With benches spread throughout and temperatures already blazing, it was a shaded, less noticeable seat that drew me.

"Mind if I share your bench?" I inquired.

"Not at all. Just people watching. Name's Laverne," he said with an outstretched arm.

"Abbie. Nice to meet you."

We small-talked for some time, spanning topics from the difficult economy to unprecedented war, during which a few apparently familiar friends trickled in. Joe introduced himself as the dishwasher at the Italian restaurant on Bay Street. As he stared at his phone a few minutes later, however, he explained that he'd been waiting seven months and six days to get a callback for another shift. Crew made a flashier entrance and rolled in on a rusty orange bike with "beat-up tires that never go flat." He was jazzed about his new haircut and talked ecstatically about turning fifty-two next week. Somewhere in this mix, I became keenly aware of how refreshing it was *to sit with people*, even if they were strangers.

At two different points, corny men approached and bluntly asked the guys if they "knew where they'd go if they died this afternoon." I never did understand why they didn't try to sell *me* salvation, but I was content to observe, nonetheless. My benchmates played along well and even politely entertained the shiny brochures and departing words of "Just believe and you'll be saved."

I didn't say anything after the first intrusion, but when the second guy left, I kind of lost it and felt the need to apologize. "I'm a Christian too and don't understand how people get off treating Jesus like that, like He's some slot machine or guilt-driving jerk who talks about hell and sinning all the time." They let me have my vent but chuckled through most of it.

"Abbie-girl, don't sweat it," Joe said sympathetically. "You'd be surprised how down in the dumps I've been, and outta nowhere comes one of those yahoos sayin' God loves me and life's gonna be okay. Hard to hate 'em too much at that point. And the truth is, usually my days do somehow get brighter after they leave."

Laverne piped in with a quick follow-up: "Long as nobody goes bringin' my mama into it, they can say whatever they want." We all laughed.

Morning came and went, and at some point I decided to move on. Laverne stood to give me a hug. "Come back and visit sometime, will ya? And when you need a place to crash, you know where the open door is."

Few moments have found me with a greater sense of longing, or belonging, or realization that home can be found in places less formal than four walls and a roof—like on a bench, I guess.

Often we Christians think that because of the Cross and being healed of any pre-Fall remnants, we should now need none but Jesus—that somehow God should be enough for our every need. But that's not true, or at least He never said it was. Jesus was alone at times, sometimes intentionally (see Matthew 14:13,23; John 6:15) and sometimes not (see Matthew 26:36-39). He *felt* alone and lonely and, as a result, sought His Father in prayer. But He also sought connection with friends.[2]

Before the "picking from the tree" bit ever happened, people weren't meant to be alone. In Genesis 2, Adam experienced loneliness and isolation as a solitary individual. His needs could not be addressed in and of himself, nor in himself plus God, creatures, and all of creation. He needed an *other*. Something about Adam's fulfillment came through relationship with Eve—through openness to another human who was both other and same. Similarly, in Mark 1:13, we see Jesus Himself distraught in the wilderness and finding strength and solace from angels.

Our primary relationship shall be with the Godhead, three in one. And our primary model of such communion and union finds us back at the image of the triune God. No anything will ever fulfill my everything, except the relationship for which I was made. To say a solo, private relationship with God is *enough* simply doesn't do justice to the created order. In the garden, before the Fall, Adam's unhindered friendship with God didn't capture the whole picture of humanity's story. It didn't capture God's intended story for humankind's existence. Man wasn't meant to be alone, even alone and in a perfect friendship with God. We were meant for more. We were made to participate in a more dynamic whole, including relationships and families, tribes and nations. We were designed for community, created to come alive in a context called the Body.

FOR FURTHER MUSING AND DISCUSSION

1. What comes to mind when you think about spending time alone? Do you enjoy it, resist it, abhor it? Why?

2. How about the idea of community? Have you ever been in a meaningful community, and, if so, what was that like for you? If not, maybe being in community, or "doing life with other people," strikes you as scary, intimidating, or threatening. How so?

3. What was a new idea for you to consider in this chapter? How could you walk that out in a practical way this week?

Because the Christian God is not a lonely God, but rather a communion of three persons, faith leads human beings into the divine communion. One cannot, however, have a self-enclosed communion with the Triune God — a "foursome," as it were — for the Christian God is not a private deity. Communion with this God is at once also communion with those others who have entrusted themselves in faith to the same God. Hence one and the same act of faith places a person into a new relationship both with God and with all others who stand in communion with God.

MIROSLAV VOLF, *After Our Likeness*

CHAPTER 4

BODILY SPEAKING

The God who is Divine community is known only in human community.

DAVID BENNER

I have community with others and I shall continue to have it only through Jesus Christ. The more genuine and the deeper our community becomes, the more will everything else between us recede, the more clearly and purely will Jesus Christ and his work become the one and only thing that is vital between us.

DIETRICH BONHOEFFER

Either we can live as unique members of a connected community, experiencing the fruit of Christ's life within us, or we can live as terrified, demanding, self-absorbed islands, disconnected from community and desperately determined to get by with whatever resources we brought to our island with us.

LARRY CRABB

IT OFTEN FEELS as if the church is *waiting* for me to get married. Ministries created for singles often feel like a waiting room (or worse, I've heard them called meat markets) whose purpose is to herd me into the next phase of life. Not only do I dislike being folded into a "singles" pile (it reminds me of when I was fourteen and had to sit at the kids' table for Thanksgiving dinner) but I also don't feel as though separate piles facilitate an intergenerational approach. When I first started caring about spiritual stuff, I attended a "separate piles" church and loved it. I credit it for much of who I am today. It was siloed into groups based on age and stage of life, and it preached an "A + B = C" gospel. For example, I was told that if I delighted myself in the Lord (singles' translation: behave/look/become a certain way), I'd soon bypass the singles' ministry and hit my next point on the holiness line: marriage. And I suppose this is appealing—being told that if you act this way, you'll turn out like this, or if you invest in this area, you'll reap that. That's why many are drawn to religion. But what happens when routes of A and B don't ever find me at the supposed C?

Nineteenth-century Englishwoman Florence Nightingale is considered the pioneer of modern nursing. What's interesting, though, is that at a young age, Nightingale sensed a call from God toward nursing but never felt connected enough to the church to figure out how the two could go together. She said the following about the Church of England:

> I would have given her my head, my heart, my hand. She would not have them. She did not know what to do with them. She told me to go back and do crochet in my mother's drawing room; or, if I were tired of that, to marry to look well at the head of my husband's table. You may go to the Sunday school, if you like it, she said. But she gave me no training even for that. She gave me neither work to do for her, nor education for it.

If you asked me to define the role of singles in the church, I'd say something like this:

> Put on then, as God's chosen ones, holy and beloved, compassionate hearts, kindness, humility, meekness, and patience, bearing with one another and, if one has a complaint against another, forgiving each other; as the Lord has forgiven you, so you also must forgive. And above all these put on love, which binds everything together in perfect harmony. And let the peace of Christ rule in your hearts, to which indeed you were called in one body. And be thankful. Let the word of Christ dwell in you richly, teaching and admonishing one another in all wisdom, singing psalms and hymns and spiritual songs,

with thankfulness in your hearts to God. And whatever you do, in word or deed, do everything in the name of the Lord Jesus, giving thanks to God the Father through him. (Colossians 3:12-17)

And maybe I'd add, "A new commandment I give to you, that you love one another: just as I have loved you, you also are to love one another" (John 13:34).

If you asked me to define the role of marrieds in the church, I'd say the same. But in practice, at least, many churches disagree.

Church makes an impression on us. Whether it's four walls, a company of congregants, or a "Turn or Burn" bumper sticker, church and its fringes cause us to think thoughts and conjure associations with God. And as a single in this mix, these impressions (of us or from us) aren't always pretty. The average American church targets the family of 2.5 kids and a white picket fence. Not only do families like this not exist but such a focus assumes marriage and biological procreation and thus neglects those of us who are not in this category (namely, all unmarried non-procreators, not to mention *the* unmarried Procreator). According to Dennis Guernsey, director of the marriage and family counseling program at Fuller Seminary, "The church's conjugal focus, that is, its focus on marriage as the core of its family ministry, systematically excludes those who are not married, giving them a sense of alienation at worst and a sense of not belonging at best."[1]

A word search of *partiality* (showing bias, relating to a part rather than the whole) in the Bible reveals that God has some thoughts on it—a lot of thoughts. *Injustice* and *impartiality* are used over and over in tandem, inviting the conclusion that showing partiality in our lives is somehow unjust. And the scary reality is that this is how singles are treated (and usually treat themselves): as incomplete and insufficient, unsure as to how they relate to the whole.

Neglecting one part or overamplifying another ends up hurting everyone. We're "not [to] pervert justice or show partiality" (Deuteronomy 16:19, NIV), "for with the LORD our God there is no injustice or partiality" (2 Chronicles 19:7, NIV). By neglecting any part of the whole, we nourish all parts of the whole's perversion. Undervaluing singleness as a complete and completely acceptable vocation and existence is unjust and, frankly, lends similar injustice to the value of marriage. Furthermore, singleness has vast capacities to point us beyond earthly marriage (and earthly sex) and bear witness to a life beyond this one — to a heavenly life. It lends itself to a high and unique invitation to give oneself to God, who enables us to give ourselves to others.

Singles can offer a divine state of existence from which marrieds have a lot to learn:

> In the Church today we need single men and women of profound spiritual depth who, out of the resources of their own interior life with the Lord, live as other Christs in the world and radiate that power to a population hungry for true Christian formation. Singles do have a mission in life to fulfill, a special yet foundational task fashioned for them by God. No matter how narrow or expansive their circumstances, no matter how limited or gifted their ability, they can and must radiate a meaning no other person can give to the world in present and future times.
>
> Of course, it will be difficult. Single spiritual living was never meant to be easy. We need only to witness the agony of Christ to understand the pain we may have to endure. But we have a promise in which to believe. And, more than that, we have a Single Person who lived as one of us, who laid down His life for all of us.[2]

Our challenge in the modern church is to move toward a separate but equal, distinct but nondisparaging relationship between married people and those who are not; widowed people and those who are not; prodigal, divorced, elderly, special needs, abused, abusive, addicted people and those who are not. Paul's first letter to the city of Corinth talks extensively about this idea, as it relates to the church being a conglomeration of parts and the necessity for every member to know his or her role, should the whole expect to function (see 1 Corinthians 12:1-27).

> We know in part and we prophesy in part, but when the perfect comes, the partial will pass away. When I was a child, I spoke like a child, I thought like a child, I reasoned like a child. When I became a man, I gave up childish ways. For now we see in a mirror dimly, but then face to face. Now I know in part; then I shall know fully, even as I have been fully known. (13:9-12)

Consider the following thoughts from author and friend Jerry Root, shared during an e-mail exchange:

> I think churches fail the single population due to a misunderstanding of unity. Some, I fear, confuse uniformity and unity. These two things are very different. Uniformity expects everyone to look and act the same, to embrace common cultural values, perhaps even a common ethnicity and language, and singles don't quite fit a uniform — everybody looks the same — model. The church is not called to uniformity but to unity. The illustration of the body as Paul used the image is significant. A body is a single organism made up of many united, but not uniform, parts. Remember, "If all were eyes, where would the hearing be?" Uniformity is usually a result of pathology and is often an accommodation to some leader's dysfunction. Everybody must conform to the leader's expectations. And the leader may or may not be in a formal leadership role. I've seen churches with a pathological uniformity, and it is no fault of the pastor but rather the result of a church power broker who holds sway unofficially. I've also seen pastors who have been the cause of the uniformity. The bottom line is that someone, through his or her own dysfunction, keeps at play a pathological and unhealthy uniformity where each is supposed to look like the others. Uniformity is a symptom of deeper pathologies. Unity, on the other hand, would be indicated by families accepting singles and singles accepting families, old accepting young and young appreciating old.

A day is promised where justice will reign and impartiality will be no more—where Love's story will trump every partial one. And cleaning up the bride in the meantime requires the messy process of learning, knowing, loving, and integrating our separate, equal stories.

Some singles idolize marriage and treat it as the ultimate goal; some marrieds are stuck searching for the idealized marriage they for so long idolized. So, in some way, we're all "partial" on this side of heaven—even those who marry. We all stumble as we walk down the aisle toward Home. I'm thankful Love doesn't. God refers to the church as His bride—not His sick, twisted, incomplete, or naked bride, until dressed in unity, but His bride. Period. She is holy, and we are she. No part is greater. No voice is insignificant. And all parts make the only whole. Maybe being the Body isn't about making all our parts one but rather learning to see one Body in all our parts.

What if every aspect of the Body was treated as crucial to the whole (see Colossians 3:14; Romans 12:4-5)? And as individuals, what if we realized that something of our longing for companionship will always be more about bonding within the Body than between two people (see 1 Corinthians 12:27; Ephesians 3:6; Colossians 3:15)? Instead of continuing to fill with false fillers, like settling for marriage simply to be married or settling for sex simply because we want it, I wonder what it would look like to implore and explore our hearts, asking what it means to be dependent and whole *as Christ's*, in union with Christ's body?

FOR FURTHER MUSING AND DISCUSSION

1. How do you think the church in general does when it comes to caring for the needs and desires of singles? What's been your experience as a single in the church?

2. What's encouraging to you about the following paragraph? Or does it seem frustrating, overwhelming, or untrue?

Singleness has vast capacities to point us beyond earthly marriage (and earthly sex) and bear witness to a life beyond this one — to a heavenly life. It lends itself to a high and unique invitation to give oneself to God, who enables us to give ourselves to others. Singles can offer a divine state of existence from which marrieds have a lot to learn.

Two Kinds of Jesus

Jesus the Band-Aid:

"I'm hurting."

Suck it up; cover it and stand tall. Strength will hold back your
tears — don't cry.

"I feel like an addict."

You are a saved sinner; move beyond your weakness — it doesn't
matter anymore. Only then can you be holy, for I am holy.

"I'm tired."

Do unto others and die unto yourself. They need you; you need to
give them your life.

"I thought I was supposed to be fixed."

You are — I saved you — and you need to start living that way. Go
and make — please get over yourself and go and make.

Jesus the Savior:

"I'm hurting."

Stay weak; expose your need and kneel. It's your pathway to
strength — I weep with you.[1]

"I feel like an addict."

You are an addicted saint; lean into your weakness — it is where my
love is. Only there can you be holy, for I am holy.[2]

"I'm tired."

Do unto yourself as you do unto others. I will take care of them; you
can step away and be with me.[3]

"I thought I was supposed to be fixed."

I saved you from death, but never from needing my love. Come
home to me — keep moving into the riches of your true self —
I am waiting.[4]

CHAPTER 5

SPIRITUAL ORGASMS

All great works are prepared in the desert, including the redemption of the world. The precursors, the followers, the Master Himself, all obeyed or have to obey one and the same law. Prophets, apostles, preachers, martyrs, pioneers of knowledge, inspired artists in every art, ordinary men and the Man-God, all pay tribute to loneliness, to the life of silence, to the night.

A. G. SERTILLANGES

MY NON-JESUS-Y FAMILY has always been supportive of my following Jesus. The topic they struggle most to understand, however, is the dating one. My dad finds it sophomoric *not* to live with someone before vowing to live with that person for the rest of one's life, and both of my parents find me far too exclusive for narrowing my pool to just Christians. I've simply had to realize that there will always be things a nonbiblical marriage will never understand about mine, and vice versa. It's still not easy, though.

I remember exaggerating profusely one recent Christmas break about a guy I'd been hanging out with. Given a combination of mistletoe and pressure from my family, I wasn't about to entertain my solo carol. So I created another one, or just added a few lyrics to the one I already had. And I've gotta say, at least for the time I was with my family, I felt a lot better about my single state. At least I could have a love story too, even if it were partially made up.

This Christmas finds me with yet another hoop to jump through.

43

I'm not only *the single one* but also *the single one without child*. My first niece, Avery, is beautiful and more than I ever could've dreamed of for my sister. But she also writes another layer to the love story that tells me my love story is lacking. What have I provided for my family? What do I have to show for my adult status?

A gal I meet with to offer spiritual direction encountered her quarter-century birthday last month. Instead of a celebratory session, however, it was exceptionally sad. In summary, she had distinct expectations for where she would be at this point in her life, and they were far from her reality.

"Help me understand what you mean by that," I requested.

"I mean a lot of things. I mean I'm not married. I mean I have no children. I have a job, but not a stable or steady one, and I'm not even positive I want to keep it or even stay in the field. I feel close to my family in some ways but also like I shouldn't be because I'm supposed to be a grown-up now. I've never had sex. I've never even had a real date. I mean I'm a letdown to society. I don't know how to make a casserole or bake a homemade pie. I don't know how to do my taxes or do laundry without messing up clothes every few loads. I don't know what the point of me is. I've spent twenty-five years as something other than dust, but that's all I feel like [dust]. I have nothing to say for my two and a half decades. He/she/it gave me a chance, and look what I've done for it: nothing."

"Who is he/she/it again?"

"Society."

"Okay, and what would it look like not to let he/she/it down?"

"I don't know. I guess I'd know who I was and where I was going. I'd be married and have at least one kid and maybe another on the way. I'd own a home and meet with women in my neighborhood for book club. I'd understand finances and have balanced perspectives on life and God and money and all the stuff you're supposed to know at my age."

"Supposed to know?"

"Yeah."

"According to who?"

"I don't know. All the other people who seem to get it."

This conversation reminded me of a recent morning when I woke to a single soliloquy spanning my girliest, loneliest, love-craving memory to that point. No matter how shallow and ungodly it seemed, all I wanted was for a man to tell me I was beautiful, and if he had a ring in hand or was named Ben or Jerry, my answer was yes. These feelings were shocking and depressing enough, but they weren't even the most pervasive. The feeling I felt most strongly that morning was anger. I was angry at God, angry at my circumstances, angry at my anger. And beneath this, I realized, were deeper layers of guilt. I felt guilty about where I was, apologizing to God that I wasn't married and had no children. As phrases hit the pages of my journal and further inwardness came out, it felt as though I were listening to someone else. But it also felt astonishingly familiar and vulnerable and *true*. Facing the reality of ourselves can be excruciating—freeing, at times, too, but the excruciation part usually comes first.

Singleness wasn't a trendy theme in Bible times, but Jephthah's daughter is one case worth mentioning, blurry though her story is. We're told she was destined for singleness because she knew she was going to die soon, so she begged her father, "Grant me this one request. . . . Give me two months to roam the hills and weep with my friends, because I will never marry" (Judges 11:37, NIV). Details of the roaming are left untold, which leaves me roaming with questions of what the lament entailed.

Did she pick married or single friends to go away with? (Because Lord knows, I struggle with jealousy toward friends who were once comrades on the single journey and then fell in love and asked me to be a bridesmaid.) Did she really grieve for two straight months? How was she changed? How much did she censor her griping and see her dependence on friends as dependence on God? Although these questions remain unanswered, we can conclude from this story that there are times for all seasons in the Christian life, grief and lament included (see Ecclesiastes 3). And, God willing, the difficult seasons will reap laughter in days to come.

Nothing of our hearts should be off-limits to God. There is no space or dream or destination to which we can travel apart from God's presence (see Psalm 139:7-8). He can rectify worst moments and remedy weakest frailties. He knows what you've told Him and what you're ashamed to tell. He knows where you're hurting and where you're afraid. And as with Jephthah's daughter, perhaps, He can meet you there.

For some of us, faith is sometimes based on what might be called spiritual orgasms — taking us from emotional high to emotional high. When I first began following Jesus, I couldn't get enough of the sensation I felt when opening the Bible or being in a room surrounded by so many other people who were similarly wanting this new way of life. I immersed myself in every book and sermon and mission trip I could get my hands on, and I wanted more. Looking back, I have meaningful memories of this season — a time when God's presence felt near and euphoric to me. But I also look back and realize that my motivations (let alone theological foundations) weren't always as solid as they seemed.

Any tint of a frown seemed bad, faithless, and fallen, while smiles were praised as good, faithful, and saved. I was polished on the outside, lending no hint of needing help. I was a warrior (see Judges 6:12) for God's kingdom, committed to fighting the good fight, going and making disciples (see Matthew 28:19) until all had heard the gospel. Hard times would hit, but I would convince myself that when I was weak, then I'd be strong (see 2 Corinthians 12:10). I fought harder and reached higher, all the while being sung to by a quiet dirge.

These beginning days of belief were like an additive, I guess, or maybe a preservative. Becoming a follower of Jesus added to who I already was but required little to no loss — or recognition — of who I wasn't. It was less about being saved from anything and more about expanding my spiritual horizons. Jesus seemed inspiring and an accessory of sorts who didn't cost me anything. Aha moments came left and right; I'd open the Bible and feel as though I'd opened Pandora's box. Verses such as "If anyone wishes to come after Me, he must deny himself, and take up his cross and follow Me" (Matthew 16:24, NASB) seemed obviously for another era. And stories such as the prodigal son (see Luke 15:11-32) were foreign to me, with themes of rebellion, sorrow, and repentance. Although the Cross seemed an incredible offer to *really* lost people, for me it didn't seem as if Jesus had to be quite that extreme. Christianity should be about gaining a better, easier, more enjoyable life. I was saved, so I had no time for feelings other than *rejoicing and being glad* (see Psalm 118:24). Beneath my shiny veneer, however, I knew that I was just a fragile piece of porcelain and that if anyone ever found a way to get near me, I'd break. And after many attempts at moral perfection, I finally broke.

Formerly bolstering nutrients of my faith began fading away, as if in a subtle weaning of sorts. I found myself frustrated by God. I asked Him why He didn't seem to pay attention to me even though He helped everyone else. Why did He tend to "sick" people but didn't dote on us "healthy" ones (see Luke 5:31)? I'd spent my whole life *not* being rebellious, slaving away in order *not* to burden Him, and He seemed stuck on those who did the reverse: those wanting rescue and willfully admitting their brokenness. Stuck in horrid fears of myself alongside horrid misunderstandings of God, however, I questioned whether such feelings were even allowed.

Clearly the story of Mary and Martha was one I'd yet to hear:

> As they went on their way, Jesus entered a village. And a woman named Martha welcomed him into her house. And she had a sister called Mary, who sat at the Lord's feet and listened to his teaching. But Martha was distracted with much serving. And she went up to him and said, "Lord, do you not care that my sister has left me to serve alone? Tell her then to help me." But the

Lord answered her, "Martha, Martha, you are anxious and troubled about many things, but one thing is necessary. Mary has chosen the good portion, which will not be taken away from her." (Luke 10:38-42)

Like Martha's, my capacities for caring about people and carrying the load myself became too heavy to handle. By God's grace, I eventually lost the strength to be strong anymore. Arduously going and making (see Matthew 28:19) for so long humbled me to a deep craving of wanting to *stay and be made.* Years removed from first putting my faith in Christ, I realized I was broken and needed something of ongoing saving (see Galatians 2:20).

My early days as a Christian marked a season full of romantic "theophanies," or manifestations of God. These are meaningful gifts, until one starts expecting them, or they start defining one's relationship. Just as orgasms weren't made to maintain a marriage, romance (though wonderful) wasn't made to be the basis of love.

So the next few years were spent slowing down, seeking a faith that flows from the inside (see Matthew 23:26), themed by something of "the way in is my only way out." I began learning about the ancient practice of spiritual disciplines and how the Spirit uses the likes of retreats and solitude, spiritual direction and prayer as means of growing us toward Himself and toward our true selves. Days were rarely easy, though. More often they felt raw and capricious, like peeling off a multilayered scab. Band-Aids work wonders for a while, I realized, but eventually they fall off or bleed through. Mine did both. Little did I know that a decade-long battle with eating disorders and different forms of anxiety had been my heart's way of screaming for liberation. Little did I know that the distance between my head and my heart had been so monstrous. I knew a lot in my head, but the distance between my head and my heart seemed to grow increasingly long.

I remember the first time I saw this distance. I'd just hung up the last of four phone calls, which had reached four answering machines, and felt striking relief, almost giddiness. Not because I could rest my sore dialing finger or had dialed more people than expected but because *no one picked up*. I was set free from actually talking to anyone but could maintain my image of being the caring person who called and said nice things to an electronic voice. I got my way, and I got relief. Admitting this cognitively was one thing, but interacting with its reality was entirely different.

Another time was when I stole a yoga mat. The sun shone brightly on a Saturday morning, and my post-yoga-class limbs were loosened up for a new day. The better news, though, was that while leaving the studio, I'd acquired a new mat.

"Finders keepers, losers weepers," I sung in my head. "So long $19.99 sucker from Target that always makes me slip." This new mat was posh and sturdy and made in Malaysia. But my soundtrack was cut short when bragging of the story to my sister, Courtney, the next day.

"You what?! You took that from the lost and found, Abb! What are you thinking!? That's somebody else's mat . . . a good mat. And they're probably a wreck about losing it."

"Umm . . . oh, I . . . uh, thought you'd be excited. I was thinking that somebody lost something and I found it, so now it's mine. Their loss, my gain kinda thing?"

"As if the lost and found is for everyone's free taking?!" she exclaimed.

"Yeah," I said hesitantly, still hoping to find the loophole that made me right. "Exactly."

Much to my dismay, the conversation joined a kitchen-wide conversation a few hours later, inviting a wider critique on my apparently pilfering ways (for which my shame gauge was rising). And although, yes, moralistic lenses concluded one could take from the lost and found as if a dumpster of pearls to bless the public, that wasn't the purpose of the lost and found. In short, I saw something better than what I already had, and I wanted it. So I took what wasn't mine. I stole a yoga mat.

These glimpses of my inward poverty were a step in the right direction, but the remaining journey seemed inestimable. The more I looked inward, the more disenchanted I became. The realities of my heart—the honest profession of my inclinations, motivations, and masks—were daunting. Chasms between "good" and "bad," or "them" and "me," started to shrink and flood over to the degree that former *ideas* from God's Word, like *all falling short* (see Romans 3:23) and God's grace being my sole sufficiency (see 2 Corinthians 12:9) began morphing into the most savory and life-saving *truths* I'd ever heard.

Then there was this random day. For no better word choice, I'll call it "the day I started caring about myself." And that's really all and everything it was. I think it was a Thursday, while I was doing my taxes or some other nonglamorous activity, when something in my being sensed a radical shift. It was as though something in me met the child in me. Grown-up Abbie rekindled with little Abbie. I felt free but guarded, alone but somehow *with*, realizing that I was nothing more and everything plus, a young, tender child longing to be loved and told she is beautiful. And when this part of me woke up and this little girl was found worthy and wanting of my explorations, I started being gentle on myself—*wanting* to be gentle on myself. *I started loving myself,* and even *liking myself,* realizing how deeply God liked me. Something in me stood taller and wanted to hear what my interior landscape was expressing because I realized my interior landscape was God's. I was God's! This day was the richest blur with heaven I'd ever tasted.

Now, before I ask you to join hands and sing "Kumbaya," hear me say that this revelatory light switch hasn't stayed on ever since. It irks me when people share stories like these and treat the Holy Spirit as if He just snaps His holy fingers and life is good. *Taste* is a significant word choice, for as much as it really was like something in me was switched on, my flesh and the Enemy still remind me of former days and coerce me into their arduous, self-condemning postures. Even on my best day, my most confident yes has the capacity to say no, and my most satisfied *right* has the capability (and proclivity by nature) to choose *wrong*. But, at the same time, I can genuinely say that something about awareness of my own worth has shifted. Though I still forget who and Whose I am, the safety of having a singleness and sexuality and sexual nature that falls under the canopy of a loving Father who calls me His own has been a worthwhile journey beyond compare.

Myths move generations more than we give credit for. You tell a guy in Africa that sleeping with the youngest virgin will cure his AIDS, and he may very well do it and tell all his tribal buddies to do it too. Or tell a kid that looking at pornography will make him popular, and he'll be on the computer 24/7. Sometimes for better, and sometimes for worse, stories shape us. Statements from parents, friends, media, and the likes play pivotal roles in how we think. That said, our pasts (experiences and relationships) hold keys to our present and future, so one of the most destructive things we do is ignore, deny, or keep secret what is true of our stories.

Some of us will explore our pasts and uncover myths or devastating wounds that have never had the chance to heal. Some of our past will be worth holding on to, some will need further counsel, and some will be worth letting go of altogether. Sexual memories, especially, are incomparable in how profoundly they affect us relationally. Looking back at our stories will be harder for some than others. Experiences such as rape or sexual abuse can taint every aspect of our lives. Even dealing with last night's bout of loneliness will require something of great courage and attention. Consolation, however, comes in knowing that a Friend (see John 15:15) and Counselor (see 14:26) is with your every dark dream and you've never been alone.[5]

Jason Mraz has a CD titled *We Sing, We Dance, We Steal Things*. This title isn't pretty, yet it's human. It doesn't justify the paradox of my being, yet it gives face to the truth of it: jubilant and pure-hearted while unjust and ego-driven in the same moment. I rationalize rules to get my way and compromise ways to create a new rule. Sometimes it frightens me to see such elementary pockets of my heart. Other times it refreshes me, permitting my paradoxes and reminding me that I never lose need for a Savior.

(And, for the record, I returned the lost yoga mat to its bin and sincerely hope the real owner finds it.)

FOR FURTHER MUSING AND DISCUSSION

1. Do you tend to be condemning or gracious with yourself? How long has this been the case? Why do you think this is the case?
2. The Scriptures talk a lot about examining what's going on inside of us (word-search *heart* to see for yourself). Try to carve out some time with God this week to check in on where your heart is. Maybe this will happen through journaling, going for a hike, or visiting a favorite secluded spot.

We are all strangers in a strange land, longing for home, but not quite knowing what or where home is. We glimpse it sometimes in our dreams, or as we turn a corner, and suddenly there is a strange, sweet familiarity that vanishes almost as soon as it comes.

MADELEINE L'ENGLE

CHAPTER 6

DATING

Many of us believe mistakenly that we should not cry at times of pain or freely acknowledge the sorrow in our hearts at death. Such a notion is not Christian. Jesus himself freely wept at the death of Lazarus, even though he knew that in a matter of moments Lazarus would live. Death was still death. Only as we acknowledge our pain and actually feel it can we begin to know healing. Only as we mourn can our mourning be turned into joy.

GORDON SMITH, *Listening to God in Times of Choice*

IF YOU ASK around, most singles will say they want to be married, and a whole lot of marrieds will say they wish they were single again, meaning one of two things: Both were sold a lie and are simply reaping its costs, or both were sold a fantastic truth but for whatever reason aren't grasping it. I think some of both might be true.

People have always tended toward love and marriage, though reasons are always shifting. Whereas one era or culture group might lack or exclude altogether romantic sides of the altar, others do the same on commitment or covenant sides. Some think society created marriage to get a handle on societal urges of sexual relations, others hold staunch beliefs of marriage as a mandate, and others consider it a rite of passage. Nevertheless, all societies have a process by which unmarried people come to be married.

In the United States, that process is predominantly personal. An unmarried person becomes attracted to, dates, and ultimately marries the person he or she has chosen. But contrary to what many people think, this so-called love story is a relatively new development. Most mate selections of the past revolved around pocketbooks and family legacy, and most decisions of marriage were made by the parents of the bride and groom. The marital union was more about linking two families than uniting two individuals.

In many cultures, men wed (usually by arrangement) women with the catch of a dowry. And women wed men (similarly by arrangement) to be financially supported and bear children. In classical Greece, fathers would betroth, or promise, daughters to their bridegroom by saying, "I pledge [girl's name] for the purpose of producing legitimate children." And woe to early wives who couldn't produce (this still goes for certain cultures today), who not only experienced personal and corporate shame but also quickly were replaced by second, third, and fourth wives until a legitimate (name-carrying) child was born. Cultural myths and aggressive treatment were rampant toward those men lacking a wife or those women lacking a fertile womb, to the degree that countless individuals have been killed on this (lacking) basis.

Up until the 1950s, by civil and religious law, husbands maintained roles as the financial provider, while women's roles revolved around sex, babies, and housekeeping. The idea of marrying for love is relatively new and not necessarily the given approach (as it can seem in the West). Theories differ, but some argue that romance as we know it started slipping into arranged marriages in England first and then sailed over the pond with the Puritans in the seventeenth century. It trickled into the middle class almost immediately and took a slower hold with the wealthier class.

When America became the land of the free, its liberties included bucking the so-called arrangement system and birthing the dating practices we know today. As of the late eighteenth century, dating had become the dominant style of the West. Not to say love and passion were absent beforehand (quite the contrary, as shown through Roman, Hebrew, and Greek letters of antiquity), but they weren't the expectation, maritally speaking, that they are today. In my great-great-grandparents' time, courtships unfolded by women initiating the "invitation to be called upon," at which point the man visited her home. If things seemed workable, they progressed from there, conducting their relationship alongside and within the context of the family (mostly the woman's).

The past hundred years have seen countless changes in the dating game and, thus, in the route to marriage. At the front end of the twentieth century, though, modern concepts of dating emerged. Courtship shifted from the privacy of a home and "went public," allowing that a male typically initiates and hosts the evening, including its financial sides, essentially "buying" his company for the night.

The rise of feminism affected roles as well. Extremes such as Eve being a biological necessity for *improving*, or even *replacing*, Adam took voice, as did more permeating ones, such as uproars within social, spiritual, educational, political, economic, and home fronts. Policies shifted (for instance, beating one's wife became illegal), as did more open approaches to equal, complementary opportunities. And, as you might imagine, with such openness came altered ideals of dating, family, love, and marriage.

Further shifting in the last twenty years has moved the norm of two-person dating into multiperson dating "groups." Looking back, I remember embryonic stages of this at my freshman homecoming in high school. Nobody asked anybody, because "we all wanted to go together." In its defense, this new way of dating grants the best of both worlds: You get "friends with benefits" but don't have to get sweaty palms over asking someone out or dealing with a breakup.

Dating today is more like hanging out and hooking up for a few months and *then* deciding whether to become boyfriend and girlfriend. Such concepts as who makes the advances and who's being pursued are absolutely vague, and sex plays into modern groups like Friday night football games. Sex has become a given—a natural next step—and is justified in that when a given relationship ends, so does the sex (usually), but it really doesn't matter because there's always someone else with whom one can hook up.[1] Whether it's sex with an actual person, or sex via a screen, there's always a noncommittal avenue nearby with which one can gratify his or her sexual urge.

I was asking my grandmother recently what it was like to communicate with her (now deceased) husband during his military stint in World War II. Though many of her answers were entirely different from what I could relate to, many were also similar: her longings for touch and the familiar voice of her lover. Or the isolating pain of waiting and wondering if what she hoped for was actually true. Clearly, technological advances such as phone, e-mail, and practically instant connection with New York, New Delhi, or Papua New Guinea at any time of the day are far different than they were in generations past. And though we may not be at a point to say whether such advancements are for better or worse, it's at least worth considering that love, as we know it, is treated quite differently.

Hollywood convinced me for a while that dating meant two strolling, skinny, hand-in-hand lovers carrying iced tall caramel macchiatos, with a fancy dog and a picnic basket overflowing with daisies. I tend to see it more like a piñata, where, blindfolded, I swing and hope on luck but miss every time, ending up empty-handed and alone. Scripture doesn't really seem to see it at all. Search *dating* in the Bible, and I promise you'll come up short. Like it or not, we've created the construct of dating. And what we've created is weird, with lots of blurry lines and suffocated attempts at relationship. "Dating well" is a sheer enigma.

I was the sixteen-year-old who gasped when a classmate tattooed Winnie-the-Pooh to her pelvic bone. All I could picture was her eighty-year-old frame and a saggy, wrinkled bear waving a red balloon. But now I'm a little different: I like tattoos.

Out with friends the other night, I noticed a mesmerizing one from across the room. The lighting was dim, so at first I couldn't make out more than a kaleidoscope of hues. But as I moved closer, the colors wrote themselves into "Ruined for Less." I rarely remember Scripture references, so if it weren't for this phrase being in the acknowledgments of my first book, I would've missed it. In Isaiah 6, the prophet describes a radical experience of coming face-to-face with God: "Woe is me, for I am ruined!" he said (verse 5, NASB), aghast that the majesties of God chose to reach out to him. And never again, he implies, may he be ruined by anything less.

This is not a tattoo coming-out party but rather a reflection on change and changed reflections and how my thinking different thoughts than I did in my driver's license era is okay. Though I don't have a tattoo, I'm keen on them now. I think they communicate a lot about an individual and mark an individuality and permanence tough to come by these days. I'm also keen on a God who's so sturdy that He's never changed (see Hebrews 13:8) and so gracious that He invites His children to change and challenge and express their growth differently today than they may have yesterday, or might tomorrow.

My deceased grandmother would roll over in her grave reading about tattoos being a means to expressing one's relationship with God, let alone a modern expression of dating and style. I suppose if we ever have grandchildren, we'll say the same about their generation's modes of expression. But that's okay, because within His order, God is okay with change and changed expressions. *He never changes.* Within His created order are ongoing expressions of creativity and redemption. Different generations say things differently, and we express ourselves differently in different seasons of our lives. I wonder what it would look like if we embraced change as crucial to becoming human instead of seeing it as conflict or conflicted identity. I think a lot of what gets us stuck as Christians is thinking that Christianity fits into a sturdy shape or tidy story. And though it has both shape and story, it is confined to neither and unfulfilled by both. God can handle our change and changing expressions. I guess the question is, can *we*?

Dating in Lincoln, Nebraska, will look different than doing eHarmony in Dallas, Texas, or downtown Manhattan, not as much because *your* style changes but because cultures' (and subcultures') styles change. And styles can be nothing more than creative reflections of diversity and personality. Consider historical shifts in styling, too. We obviously don't talk about dowries or sit around the fire telling stories about how many cows we sacrificed in order to get a spouse. Aside from a few references (Zechariah and Elizabeth, Mary and Joseph, Priscilla and Aquila), the New Testament steers clear of much verbiage about specific married couples. (Ananias and Sapphira are also mentioned, but they wound up dead due to collapsed integrity.[2])

From Scripture's perspective, Jesus' coming seems less about instruction toward what is and more about an invitation toward what is to come, now and forevermore. It's about unity and union through the Father, the Son, and the Spirit (the Spirit proceeds from the Father and will be with us forever [see John 14:16; 15:26; 16:7]). Jesus didn't offer a language of blueprint answers; He offered an eternal proposition of intimacy, compassion, and truth, washing servants' feet (see John 13:14) and welding broken hearts (see Psalm 147:3) with kindness (see Romans 2:4). And either this is still true about Him (see Zephaniah 3:17; Luke 17:21; John 16:32; Philippians 4:9; Hebrews 3:14; 10:16; Revelation 21:3) or it's not. Either the impulses that motivated Jesus' life, death, and resurrection are, in fact, alive in me today (see John 1:14; Romans 8:9-11; 2 Timothy 1:14) or they're not.

FOR FURTHER MUSING AND DISCUSSION

1. What comes to mind when you hear the word *dating*? Is it a positive, negative, neutral, or exhausted connotation?
2. Spend some time talking about this quote:

> From Scripture's perspective, Jesus' coming seems less about instruction toward what is and more about an invitation toward what is to come, now and forevermore. It's about unity and union through the Father, the Son, and the Spirit (the Spirit proceeds from the Father and will be with us forever). Jesus didn't offer a language of blueprint

answers; He offered an eternal proposition of intimacy, compassion, and truth, washing servants' feet and welding broken hearts with kindness. And either this is still true about Him or it's not. Either the impulses that motivated Jesus' life, death, and resurrection are, in fact, alive in me today or they're not.

What stands out to you? What's the hardest sentence for you to actually believe?

How Much?

How much can the heart take?

When one man's battle is another man's breeze, where is the
level to which one can hurt?

Or what is the liberty to which one should help?

Where is the level to which one can guard his "wellspring of
life"?

Or what is the end to which one should unguard his journey of
life?

If you put yourself out there, you put yourself into vulnerability.

You put yourself into the space.

The space between known and unknown.

The space between seen and unseen.

When you put yourself out there, you put yourself into
nakedness.

Into the space where shame hides.

Or hollers.

Where freedom hides.

Or hollers.

How much can the heart take?

CHAPTER 7

BREAKUPS AND DEATH

The truth is that our finest moments are most likely to occur when we are feeling deeply uncomfortable, unhappy, or unfulfilled. For it is only in such moments, propelled by our discomfort, that we are likely to step out of our ruts and start searching for different ways or truer answers.

M. SCOTT PECK

In the midst of winter I finally learned that there was in me an invincible summer.

ALBERT CAMUS

The day came when the risk to remain tight in a bud was more painful than the risk it took to blossom.

ANAÏS NIN

THERE'S NOT MUCH worse than the petal that proclaims, "Loves me not." And, sad though it is, unreciprocated loves happen more often than the reciprocated kind. I was definitely the girl growing up who'd scoff at your boy sorrows and consider your love pains lame. A few personal heartbreaks later, however, I can't think of much that's more painful. If love, or marriage, were an arrangement, coupled with a commitment, it would seem far more simple. But it's not. Today's matchmaking involves much choice and subjectivity—and usually fails. Lovely, eh? How's this for a motivating chapter intro? I know, and I apologize, but I am simply stating a fact in saying that dating relationships *usually* break up.

The first time I got mad at God was during a breakup. This guy and I had done everything "right," including following what seemed to be answers to our prayers that we should stay together. So when we broke up, it felt like God's fault. It is dangerous to presume that moving "upward" (like in the triangle picture of dating, with the couple as the two bottom points and God at the pinnacle), or toward God, will always lead the couple closer. Sometimes God breaks up two good people with two good paths for no good reason, except to draw us closer to Him.

Sharing our souls is the most vulnerable thing we can do. We're unpredictable and paradoxical and foolish and peculiar and quirky and fickle and multilayered and boring and needy and too much and not enough. So why on earth would I want to share all of *that* with another, especially when another could reject it?

"My soul can take only so many dumps," I recently told God, "or crushes, or dumped crushes, or cut-short destinations. I'm tired of putting it out there only to have it left there or be left to suffer silently. Plus, if You knew all along I'd mess up (or be messed up by) a given relationship, why did You allow it to unfold in the first place? Why do You allow, and even lead, me to date people, blessing our territories for a time yet knowing full well a breakup song is queued up? Are You *that* obsessed with my growth that You'd hurt me so deeply? Or that undone by my lacking faith that You'd punish, ignore, and play games with me? Or is there something more delicate at hand here?"

I didn't cry much as a kid, but one time I did was New Year's Eve, 1989. I was traveling with my family, lodging at a Days Inn somewhere between Charlotte and DC. As midnight approached, my young senses were tiring, yet a fresh determination empowered my eyelids. "The end" was growing close and I was growing more and more desperate to stay with 1989. It seemed the end of an era to my eight-year-old mind, and I was devastated. How could it leave? How could it depart so quickly and never come back? Was it really never coming back? I couldn't deal with it. I didn't want to deal with it. I was mad at the year—angry that it would enter my life so richly yet hold the audacity to depart. Tears poured as on television the Times Square ball dropped. I simultaneously made every effort to save the year by scooping its last breaths into an empty salad-dressing bottle. In a flash, 1989 was gone. Death had confronted me. And, like death, even when expected, breakups are unnatural, unexpected, and painful; they taste like loss, which usually recalls other tasted losses. And they make us feel as though we have been lost.

One of the biggest tragedies in our breakup sagas is when we trivialize their processes to "natural." I become a slave to my pain when I try to narrow its comprehensions to "logic." Hovering beneath Christian jargon and hiding our authentic, God-given judgment hides us from reality. Some days will be hard (like when you want to console, or be consoled by, an ex), and some situations are plain awkward (like seeing an old crush or seeing a new one with your old best friend). The alternative, however, is to stuff our pain in such statements as "I know God, so I shouldn't be upset" or "God always has a happy plan and future for me, so I've just gotta suck it up and move on." Truth never modeled such a tale. To risk having one's feelings hurt or handing over your real feelings will usually be hard. But if God is true and truly lords over all seen and unseen intricacies (including feelings), we're better off being authentically upset, heartbroken, and maybe even awkward than maturing a lie.

God is all about holiness—showing us ours and drawing us toward His—so much so, in fact, that Scripture says His overarching will for our lives is holiness (see 1 Thessalonians 4:1-8; 1 Peter 1:15). But what about when holiness doesn't fix us or necessarily make us feel happy? And why is it that holiness seems to come more often through the likes of heartbreaks and breakups than in a smooth-sailing life? Although sometimes holiness involves happiness, other times it involves suffering, unfulfilled longing, and societal persecution. Even in this, however, what's challenging to believe is that God is good and has your best interests in mind (see Romans 8:28).

When asked why I trust a deity who has the power to take everything away, I've realized there's actually no other deity I'd rather trust. Being in authentic relationships means I will hurt and get hurt. The paradox and miracle here, however, is that getting hurt is a guaranteed gateway between God and my soul. Tragedy opens me to transformation. Maybe that's why broken people are so quick to profess nearness to Jesus (see Luke 6:20): Broken people aren't scared to admit needs, such as longing and rescue.

We've become so jaded to the simplicity and profundity of the Trinity's Love story that we usually lose sight of its intended end and told beginning. We forget that God is the essence of true art, beauty, glory, sex, truth, identity, creation, order, and mystery (see Job 5:9; Ecclesiastes 3:11; Isaiah 40:28; Romans 11:33). We forget that He heals the broken heart, not the unbroken one; that His love fills an empty form, not a full one. We are orphans (see Exodus 22:21; 23:9; Deuteronomy 10:19; Hebrews 11:13; 1 Peter 1:1; 2:11), but we have also been found (see 2 Samuel 14:14; Jeremiah 20:13; John 14:18; Ephesians 2:19; James 1:27). God's way is always love (see 1 John 4:8) — severe at times, yes, and certainly not easy, painless, clear, exportable, balanced, relevant, accepted, admired, foreseeable, predictable, precise, timely, or simple but always deeply packed in love. We forget that He's focused on union and unifying our hearts back to His — back to the heart of who we really are, in Him, as His, toward Love. We forget that He is worth trusting.

Either God is good and for our good and knows what He is about or He doesn't. Either pain and death are the end of our stories or they're not. Successful dating should not be classified only as those who "get hitched." Successful dating, or courtship, or *life*, that is, happens when a man and a woman are moved closer to God. Even in courtships that break up or unrequited love that never requites, God's hand is still initiating and pursuing and making something new. "Naked [we] came from [our] mother's womb, and naked shall [we] return. The LORD gave, and the LORD has taken away; blessed be the name of the LORD" (Job 1:21). We make messy attempts toward life and love, usually with even messier results. And for some reason, God lets us—and loves us all throughout. Though difficult to recognize at times and more difficult to receive, He is always shaping a rescue story, always telling us our story of being made clean (see John 15:3). The question is, are we willing to listen?

FOR FURTHER MUSING AND DISCUSSION

1. What's been your experience of breakups? In other words, how have breakups affected your life and relationship with exes, God, or yourself (relief, guilt, hatred, anger, self-hatred)?
2. God promises that in all things, He's working out a plan not only for His good, but ours (see Romans 8:28). How does that correlate with this chapter and maybe even what you answered in question 1?

Shame

He visited today,
In a different, yet still awful way.
Different in that I recognized him,
and awful in that recognizable or not,
he still exudes awfulness —
like a whispering ghost,
criticizing my every move.
I saw his face; I felt his disdain.
He stared at my righteous anger
and asked me to hate.
He gaped at my lingering hopes
and listed his lying answers.
He mocked my sadness,
Marked my weakness,
Masked my gladness,
And raped my good.
He marveled at my tears
and told them not to stop.
He flirted with my fatigue
and scoffed at my frame.
He grabbed me by the hand,
Gripping me toward his dance.
But I pulled away, saying,
"I see you today, and your story is not worth my time."

CHAPTER 8

SUBMISSION AND BEAUTY

The woman was made of a rib out of the side of Adam; not made out of his head to rule over him, nor out of his feet to be trampled upon by him, but out of his side to be equal with him, under his arm to be protected, and near his heart to be beloved.

MATTHEW HENRY

A woman's heart should be so hidden in God that a man has to seek Him just to find her.

MAYA ANGELOU

As in one body we have many members, and the members do not all have the same function, so we, though many, are one body in Christ, and individually members one of another. Having gifts that differ according to the grace given to us, let us use them.

ROMANS 12:4-6

SUBMISSION IS NOT a word we like to mention. Even in church circles, it makes most squirm—or cuss—and is rarely a topic mentioned by singles. Yet God has been making mention of it since day one. Just as we find mutual expressions of love and submission in relations of God the Father, Jesus the Son, and the Holy Spirit, so we have been invited into such expressions. For a number of reasons, though (involving pride, forgetfulness, rebellion, and abuse), we tend to settle for lesser invitations.

In Ephesians 5, before Paul introduced the infamous words about wives submitting to their husbands, he wrote of being filled with the Spirit, addressing one another in psalms and hymns and spiritual songs, singing and making melody to the Lord with our hearts, giving thanks always and for everything to God the Father in the name of our Lord Jesus Christ, and *submitting to one another out of reverence for Christ* (see verses 18-21). The Christian life should continually bear a posture of submission, kneeling at the greatness of our God. Love translates to sacrifice, and sacrifice translates to submission, as told and lived by the Godhead Himself, who *submitted Himself to death* (see Isaiah 53:12), *even death on a cross* (see Philippians 2:8), providing the greatest act of sacrifice (see Hebrews 9:26) and love (see John 3:16; 15:13; 1 John 4:7,19) in all of humanity.

Genesis 1:26-28 introduces man and woman being made separately, yet both in God's image and with dominion over God's creation. Man and woman were created different but mutual, unique but cooperative, like apples and oranges, with different tastes, textures, and personalities, but equal in value as fruits—and grounded in love. Adam was made head over Eve, not in a sense of value but role. Likewise, man came from God (see Genesis 2:7) and woman from man (see Genesis 2:22-23) so that man is ultimately submissive to the Godhead, and woman to man and the Godhead (see 1 Corinthians 11:3,8-9). Furthermore, man has been created with the privilege of pursuing the woman, and woman with the privilege of honoring the man (see Ephesians 5:22-31). And cooperation herein, with unique roles and submissions, evokes our fullest dimensions of love and freedom.

On the flip side, avoidance, or ignorance, of the created order is destructive. Women feel isolated and alone, and men feel emasculated (sinking into passivity), further eliciting the "Eve nature" to step up and lead/create/speak out of line. Women end up less than fulfilled, further hidden behind layers of strength and an attitude of "It's fine; I'm okay; I don't need any help," when deep down part of us craves validation in our fragility and longs for guidance, protection, and a shoulder to lean on.

As long as I'm single (whether it's a season or my entire earthly lifetime), God invites me to seek such validation, guidance, and protection from spiritual fathers and brothers in my midst (see 1 Peter 5:5).[1] In doing so, not only does this enable men to be men, edifying them toward their designed masculinity, but it also enables women to function most radiantly in our beauty, coming from our created order under the kind strength of the rib from which we came.

Some years back, I was reading a book about beauty. On the porch during a family vacation, my mom and I sat side by side, she with Oprah's latest scoop and I working through *Do You Think I'm Beautiful?* by Angela Thomas.

"Seems neat that your generation uses that word," my mom said, catching me off guard.

"*My* generation? You mean yours didn't?"

"No . . . well, at least my piece of my generation didn't. I was made fun of when I was young; a boy called me homely once. From that point on, I decided beauty was given to some and not others. And I was a *'not other.'"*

I was heartbroken, and I didn't know what to say back to my beautiful mother. A few years later, I know a little more but am still far from grasping beauty's complexities.

Dictionary definitions refer to beauty with such words as *harmony* and *elegance, simplicity* and *brilliance,* perceived in their whole as *something beautiful.* Scripture expounds on beauty as being delicate, lasting, and far more than meets the eye. "Let your adorning be the hidden person of the heart with the imperishable beauty of a gentle and quiet spirit, which in God's sight is very precious," we're told in 1 Peter 3:4. Beauty doesn't come from being perpetually skinny or sexy. One of the most beautiful women I know is eighty-four and covered in wrinkles.

True beauty is transcendent, delighting senses and revealing things spiritual and captivating to my soul (physically, emotionally, morally, cognitively). True beauty awakens me to God, connecting me to His lasting work in my soul. And when I realize God is fascinated by my beauty, by the beauty of Himself imaged in me, I become fascinated by Him.

Lately, I've been a witness to elements of beauty in the African American culture. Living in a transitional black neighborhood, I'm slowly learning how different we are and also how alike. Some may say that neighborhood children on one street, in one city, in one state of America aren't a fair representation or credible instructor, but they've sure been making a good stand-in for me.

Tanerica came over this morning, wondering if we could read Bible stories in the side yard. She's eleven and wants to be a fashion designer. Her dad is in and out of jail, and her mom is eight months pregnant and addicted to drugs. I told her I couldn't today but promised we would soon.

"That's fine, Miss Abbie. Can I show you somethin' before you leave?"

"Sure, honey. What is it?"

"A boy from my class gave it to me," she said, pulling a wad of paper from her left pocket.

Conscientious penmanship marked the top line: "*i think ur pritty.*"

"Well, that was sweet of him, Tanerica. And he sure is right!"

Seeing the angst and wonder caused by this wad of paper, I decided to sit with her on the porch for a bit.

"Why do you think it means so much to a girl when a boy says she's pretty?" I asked. She thought for a few moments, shifting her eyes to the floor. "Maybe cuz girls think they so ugly no boy will ever say they pritty." Another handful of moments passed before Tanerica asked, "Does God say ur pretty, Miss Abbie?"

"He does, sweetheart, all the time."

"Why?"

"Because I forget, and He knows sometimes I need to be reminded about how He made me and why He thinks I'm beautiful."

"You think God can tell me that, Miss Abbie?"

"I know He can tell you that, Tanerica. Why don't you come over tonight and we'll read about what God thinks."

"Okay."

Women are the last mentioned in God's created order — and arguably the most complex of His creativity, in a phenomenal sort of way. Even before the Fall, God knew that man was missing a vital aspect of health and pleasure. It was through the satisfying companionship, radiant beauty, and captivating soul of another, then, that He would put His finishing touch on the design of man. "She shall be called Woman" (Genesis 2:23). As from God stemmed man, so from man stemmed his cherished sister, woman. "Then the LORD God formed the man of dust from the ground and breathed into his nostrils the breath of life, and the man became a living creature" (verse 7). "And the rib that the LORD God had taken from the man he made into a woman and brought her to the man" (verse 22). "And the man and his wife were both naked and were not ashamed" (verse 25).

And God found her stunning (see Song of Solomon 4:7).

All beautiful you are, my darling; there is no flaw in you. (NIV)

You are altogether beautiful, my darling, and there is no blemish in you. (NASB)

You're beautiful from head to toe, my dear love, beautiful beyond compare, absolutely flawless. (MSG)

[He exclaimed] O my love, how beautiful you are! There is no flaw in you! (AMP)

You are altogether beautiful, my darling, beautiful in every way. (NLT)

Thou art all fair, my love; there is no spot in thee. (KJV)

You are altogether beautiful, my love; there is no flaw in you. (ESV)

It's tempting to think we women can cause our beauty, as if beauty is something tangible or exportable. But not unlike ocean waves or a newborn baby's finger, beauty transcends what mankind can create, do, or be alone. All beauty flows from beauty's Maker, God, and the only way we can alter it is by rejecting it. Yes, feeling pretty and not being in the bloated days of PMS may help, but when all is said and done, my beauty simply is. When I am me, I am beautiful, because when I am me, I am actively interacting with God's thoughtful design of me and, thus, with an essence of God. And God is beautiful. My image is made in the image of the Godhead and, therefore, in and of itself is beautiful.[2]

Desires and ideals that fall from somewhere other than the canopy of God's beauty will never survive. True beauty connects God's ways to mine, and mine to His, my only hope of glory (see Colossians 1:27). And to imitate Christ (see Ephesians 5:1-20), I am learning, is to believe this. To walk in a manner believing utmost Worth resides in me; utmost Beauty is intricately woven into my femininity and inmost being.

Our final destiny as Christians involves the purest of ecstasies. A belief and joy that is "inexpressible and filled with glory," Peter said (1 Peter 1:8). The beatific vision.[3] A day is coming when we will stand face-to-face with Christ Jesus Himself, our souls actually looking at God. God is the most beautiful Being, and we are God's kin. Logic deduces, then, that functioning as God's child, obeying the tides of His masterful creation, images the divine and documents Divinity's beauty to the world.

Most days we forget this. Most days we live more in line with the world's order than creation's. We forget who we are, and we forget that we're special—to God, among others. We forget that we're sculpted by the Hands who created creativity, truth, wonder, and beauty. We forget that singleness doesn't affect our beauty or define us. Nor does marriage, engagement, or dating. We forget that being a size (or five sizes) smaller won't shift who we are in the eyes of our Maker. It won't shift how much we're treasured and sought after by the Redeemer or change the deepest reality of who we are as daughters of the King. Most days we forget how beautiful we are and internalize the opposite. But when we do remember our beauty and the Beauty from which we stem, we naturally obey and submit to Order's fluidity, femininity, and strength. We naturally live out our sexuality.

FOR FURTHER MUSING AND DISCUSSION

1. We all come to the table with different views, ideas, and ideals of beauty and submission. Spend some minutes discussing these, not in search of a right or wrong answer but to get to know one another and yourself and to see how our backgrounds affect us.
2. Share something that was refreshing to you in this chapter.
3. "When I am me, I am beautiful, because when I am me, I am actively interacting with God's thoughtful design of me and, thus, with an essence of God. And God is beautiful. My image is made in the image of the Godhead and, therefore, in and of itself is beautiful." Do you agree? Why or why not?

I Asked the Lord by John Newton

I asked the Lord that I might grow
In faith and love and every grace.
Might more of His salvation know
And seek more earnestly His face.

'Twas He who taught me thus to pray
And He I trust has answered prayer.
But it has been in such a way
As almost drove me to despair.

I hoped that in some favored hour
At once He'd answer my request
And by His love's constraining power
Subdue my sins and give me rest.

Instead of this He made me feel
The hidden evils of my heart
And let the angry pow'rs of hell
Assault my soul in every part.

"Lord, why is this," I trembling cried,
"Wilt Thou pursue thy worm to death?"
"'Tis in this way" the Lord replied,
"I answer prayer for grace and faith.

"These inward trials I employ
From self and pride to set thee free
And break thy schemes of earthly joy
That thou mayest seek thy all in Me."

CHAPTER 9

INVOLUNTARY SINGLENESS

If I find in myself a desire which no experience in this world can satisfy, the most probable explanation is that I was made for another world.

C. S. LEWIS, *Mere Christianity*

A community is only really a community when all its members realise how deeply they need the gifts of others, and try to make themselves more transparent and more faithful in the exercise of their own gift. So a community is built by every one of its members, all in their own way.

JEAN VANIER, *Community and Growth*

SCRIPTURE IS DECORATED by covenant language, and most people get married—meaning, I guess, we're safe to assume that God *likes* marriage and that parts of marriage and covenants and altars are part of God's design for us. But what does this mean for us who are single? God said it is not good for man to be alone (see Genesis 2:18), and then some years later, Paul said it is good for man not to marry (see 1 Corinthians 7:1), leaving me to think that either the Bible has a typo or there's a less-traveled option, such as being fully *with* while *without*—fully *in communion* without communing with a ring attached to your finger and a spouse attached to your hip.

Marrieds and singles are different. When single friend Jane (or Joe) gets in a dating, engaged, or definitely married relationship, the conversation changes. Then he or she tells me, "Just hang in there, Abbie—it'll happen when you least expect it," or puts me on the defensive by saying, "I just don't understand why such a nice-looking girl like you isn't married." I want to vomit. That person made it to the other side and, I'm convinced, no longer fully understands the state of my single soul. Another single friend jokes about starting a convent called "Second to None." And though I've never thought seriously about a vow of celibacy, there have been more than a few days and nights when this invitation seemed appealing. There's something sublimely appealing about not having to deal with the mate race anymore.

In 2010, the United States Census Bureau reported that there are 99.6 million unmarried people over age eighteen in the United States, representing nearly 44 percent of the adult population.[1] Furthermore, recent decades have shown dramatic increases in the single population as well as Christian singles seeking some sort of theological backing, or understanding, about his or her state of singleness. Among the challenges here, however, is that God doesn't spend too much ink in the Bible talking about singleness. In Matthew 19, He explains that certain individuals are given the capacity to accept a nonmarried existence (see verses 10-12), and Paul spoke of his singleness, saying, "I wish that all were as I myself am. But each has his own gift from God, one of one kind and one of another" (1 Corinthians 7:7). In Judges 11:38, we see that Jephthah's daughter did not marry, and by God's command, neither did Jeremiah (see Jeremiah 16:2). Isaiah encouraged eunuchs with the hope of a hearty and everlasting inheritance and identity, provided they were faithful to God's commands (see Isaiah 56:3-5), and the prophetess Anna lived faithfully as a widow for sixty years (see Luke 2:36-37). Four virgin daughters of Philip prophesied in the early church (see Acts 21:9), while some widows made pledges to remain unmarried (see 1 Timothy 5:3-16), and 144,000 who "did not defile themselves with women" are said to appear in the Apocalypse (Revelation 14:1-5, NIV). The majority of scholars (Christ believing and not) agree that Jesus, Paul, and John the Baptist were all celibate.

Folks I've met who feel a calling to singleness, or celibate living, have come to their understanding based on personal convictions (often unrelated to a lack of desire for marriage or sex), compelled by longings for deeper union with God. And as Richard Foster said,

> We do [such] people a disservice when we fail to proclaim the single life as a Christian option. Marriage is not for everyone, and we should say so. A single person can venture into forms of simplicity that are closed to the rest of us. By word and deed the Church should encourage these faithful servants of Christ. They should never be looked down upon or viewed as somehow odd. We should do all that we can to be with those who have chosen the single life, because they need our friendship and we need their wisdom. . . . The life of St. Francis gives us a healthy model of celibacy. (Examples of unhealthy celibacy abound in the history of the Church.) This matter of the single life should not be taken lightly. To be quite blunt about it, celibacy is necessary for some forms of simplicity. Francis could not have done what he did if he had not been single. Nor could Jesus.[2]

As with any state or stage we find ourselves in, singleness does not define one's spiritual identity. That is not to say, however, that one shouldn't pursue fervent explorations herein. If someone is single and neither terribly inclined toward marriage nor in conflict with his or her sexual impulses, he or she may more naturally be led to explore vows of celibacy or an intentional life of singleness. I've met one person like this, and he's gone on to join the Benedictine order.

We've sidetracked here into explorations of celibacy, or a Christ-centered, voluntary, lifelong commitment to virginity. Involuntarily single, however, describes the vast majority of us: we who remain single for whatever reason and who, generally speaking, have the hope of becoming married. Though the former is of great importance, our focus will center on the latter—a life of involuntary celibacy, or single-ness in light of learning to follow Jesus.

Throughout history, cultures have deemed singles sexless and barren and, at times, even cursed and unable to secure their eternal placement. A baby we know as Jesus shattered this paradigm, though, or at least shifted it dramatically for Christians. Seemingly out of the blue and certainly removed from conventional wisdom, Jesus proposed the idea of salvation being based not on one's marital status, nor eternal life evolving from one's last name, but rather on following Him. Never did Jesus mention marriage in this life as a prerequisite for anything in the next. In His paradigm, rather, the nuclear family was secondary to the ever-enduring kingdom family, Body of Christ, or church. He further tweaked prejudices of marriage itself by reframing its context to one that would not carry over into heaven (see Matthew 22:30; Mark 12:25; Luke 20:35). Apparently, heaven will revolve around different preoccupations than obsessions over a mate, such as obsessions over our Maker, ecstasies of utmost inti-macy, and union with God.

The union of marriage has forever reflected a deeper union between God and His people (namely Yahweh in covenant relation-ship with Israel). Jesus brought forth a new tint on ideals, however, and His celibacy reoriented Old Testament and ancient Judaic obligations of marriage and salvation as a physical family (Israel) to a new priority of Christ's bride and our new family, the church. Grace and salvation are available through both marriage and celibacy, and marriage no longer acts as a barometer of holiness. That is, persons may be as holy in a married state as they are in a single state (see Titus 2:11-14; 3:4-7). Though both marriage and singleness carry unique values and mean-ings, Christ incarnated a theology in which both are equally valid and valuable ways of life.

Paul wrote of his decision for celibacy in 1 Corinthians 7, not forbidding marriage but clearly justifying reasons for both marriage and celibacy. On the one hand, Paul explained that those who fornicate should marry and, on the other hand, that if a dating couple can keep from having sex, they should remain single. In other words, if I might paraphrase, if you are single, for this hour, at least, God has granted you the gift of singleness (which we tend to more often consider a curse). If you are married, He has not. "Don't be wishing you were someplace else or with someone else. Where you are right now is God's place for you" (1 Corinthians 7:17, MSG).

Between the middle of the third century and the beginning of the fourth, something of an ascetic movement emerged, in part responding to an interpretation of these words from Paul: "I beat my body and make it my slave so that after I have preached to others, I myself will not be disqualified for the prize" (1 Corinthians 9:27, NIV). Emphasis on achieving God's perfection in this life caused many to renounce wealth, property, power, comfort, family, and, most of all, sex so that asceticism became a common practice. One author explained it as "the denial of the body, sexual pleasure, and repression of erotic desire, understood by the faithful to be a holy act of religious devotion required to enter God's service."[3] Suppression of desires, particularly sexual ones, became an acceptable norm, and although church leaders still identified sexual instinct as natural, they held out that sexual intercourse should take place only (for marrieds) with an end of procreation.

By the fifth century, Roman Catholics had not only declared clerical celibacy an official doctrine but also more spiritual and, in many cases, the better way. Saint Augustine's influence during these years was unrivaled. Sexual arousal of any kind was appalling to him, and he saw no difference between that which occurred in the marriage bed and that between a man and a prostitute. Sexual arousal was considered sinful by him unless strictly set in the context of marriage and toward ends of reproduction.[4] For Augustine, the ideal marriage should be purely platonic, to the extent that man should "sow his seed into his wife" without allowing any pleasure or passion to ensue. Jerome, an Augustinian contemporary, took it to yet another level, insisting that a man touching a woman, even one's wife, was evil and a sure way to break communion with God.

Moving ahead a few centuries, one finds the famous workings of Martin Luther, credited for much regarding the split between Catholics and what became Protestants. Up to this point, most church leaders were single—Augustine and Aquinas, Teresa of Avila, Thomas à Kempis, and Luther, even, at the time of nailing his Ninety-Five Theses. Luther was irritated by lost beliefs about marriage and family as being the normative and natural state. Contrary to thinkers who downplayed marriage, denigrated sex, and even urged lifelong celibacy, Luther affirmed that unless you're the rare individual who's called to a celibate life, marriage and sex are natural, necessary, and an obvious step toward procreation. He celebrated the idea of regular intercourse in a marital relationship and, even when single, didn't hesitate to speak on the virtuous nature of marriage. Many wondered whether Luther would ever marry. He did, in fact, at forty-two, creating quite the scandal when he tied the knot with twenty-six-year-old runaway nun Catherine von Bora.

> Little did the sixteenth-century world realize the tremendous significance—both religious and social—of this simple and reverent ceremony in the backwoods of rural Germany. The union of Martin and Katie was not cursed with the birth of the Antichrist. Instead, it was blessed with the birth of the Protestant parsonage and the rebirth of a genuinely Christian ethos in home and community. Luther's marriage remains to this day the central evangelical symbol of the Reformation's liberation and transformation of the Christian daily life.[5]

Since the Reformation, there's been a church focus floating between banks of "youth" and "married adults," thereby leaving a pool of ostracized singles floating (or drowning) in the middle. Throughout most of history, singles have struggled to find a home. Ask most of them, and you'll likely hear something along the lines of their singleness being their fault and, furthermore, that they are incomplete, inadequate, or insufficient in a mature, godly existence until married. Part of this is self-inflicted; most is cultural. The Scriptures and history, however, tell an entirely different story. To be in covenantal union is in our blood—in the very soul of our core design. Marrieds and singles alike are made for exclusive, covenanted, lifelong commitments and intimacy, modeled by the experience of community in the Trinity. The design of marriage sees to this through an exclusive, covenanted relationship with God and one's spouse. The design of singleness sees to this through an exclusive, covenanted relationship with God and nonexclusive bonds with friends among the Body of Christ.[6]

Scripture says that fulfillment (sexual or otherwise) does not come by marriage; fulfillment comes by Christ and His body and our dependent participation and transformation, waiting, watching, and abiding in relentless fringes of His Love. But Scripture also says there was a tragic fall that twisted every aspect of our presumed fulfillment. The terrible reality of the Fall was the tragic denial of our dependence on God. Adam and Eve partook of what God said not to. He seemed to be holding out on them, and the serpent's offerings seemed far more fruitful. Saying yes to the serpent, however, shattered perfection and shouted shame into the skin of human existence. Mankind was now naked and ashamed, vulnerable beyond belief and disjointed from our Maker.

The repercussions of this tragic rebellion remain. Experiencing life, and singleness, involves pain. Yet if God is good and true and truly for us, any angle we take on life, or singleness, must maintain invitations of eternal goodness. And any worldly end that promises such lasting goodness, whether possessions or positions, relationships or roles, must be unloosed. Though marriage will remain an utmost pining on this side of heaven, our full union with the Godhead will happen only in heaven. Marriage as we know it will be no more (see Matthew 22:30). We will continue as sexual beings through eternity and, consequently, will continue in our drive toward bonding with an *other*, but the marital foundation will cease to exist, and all covenantal energy will exist fully in relationship to the triune God.

As much as singles may not like hearing this, we have a unique opportunity to seize opportunities and union with the marital covenant of Christ—an advantage, even, compared to marrieds. I don't say this to squelch our hopes for an earthly union but simply to say that where we are is where God has us, and in this place, He is near with a handful of gifts and a unique call to a table of ecstasy. Single Christians have a prophetic and crucial voice for *all* Christians and their remembrance of a primary identity and union *with God*. We illustrate a spiritual love that ultimately binds the church and beholds the sacramental pledge of marriage.

Although it may not be the single person's favorite thought, we are, as singles, a necessary gift to the Body. Furthermore, our celibacy, even if involuntary, can lend greater capacities toward ministry and intimacies with Christ. The physical union of sex has no biblical basis for making marriage inferior to singleness, nor do the commitments of poverty, chastity, and obedience make the celibate greater. The measure of every human being's perfection is charity. Love is our utmost rule, highest call, and greatest gift. "So now faith, hope, and love abide, these three; but the greatest of these is love" (1 Corinthians 13:13). As it was in Eden and will be throughout eternity, our identity, as singles and as marrieds, resides in the kingdom of God.

A friend of mine relates singleness to disability. If you've ever met secure physically disabled people, they will typically tell you that although their impairment wouldn't have necessarily been their choice, it's become an integral part of them and their story. Many will actually say their disability has made them who they are. Similarly, I believe that singleness, like any other "thorn in our flesh" (see 2 Corinthians 12:7), has the capacity to eat us alive or become a bridge for us to truly *live alive*. We can drown our sorrows brought on by singleness, blaming and busying ourselves, acting out of its felt voids, or we can face the reality of this lot we've been dealt, including its pain and loneliness at times, and seek God in that midst. If He's really the Godhead, Savior, and friend He's proclaimed Himself, His sufficiencies will not fall short for a soul who is single.

Though statistically most of us will marry, it clearly isn't a prerequisite for holiness. You're not going to die if you stay single, and I'm not going to live happily ever after if I get married. Never having sex won't kill us, and having sex every day from now till our graves won't bring us to life. Getting married will not cure loneliness, and neither will a commitment to celibacy. Making love will not cure lust, and neither will masturbation. A spouse will never fully satisfy desires for intimacy, nor will a solo existence permit ultimate ecstasy. We were made for more.

FOR FURTHER MUSING AND DISCUSSION

1. Have you ever felt as though singleness defined you, or maybe that others treated you as if it defined you? What was that like?
2. How did Jesus' coming affect singleness?
3. How does your answer in question 2 affect and encourage you?

Love wants to be one-sided, but it's two.

You can have my glory, but there's a cost at stake too.

Love wants to be easy, but it's hard.

You can have my romance, but there's a journey standing guard.

CHAPTER 10

SACRED DIMENSIONS OF WAITING

Do not arouse or awaken love until it so desires.

SONG OF SOLOMON 2:7; 3:5; 8:4 (NIV)

What will it profit a man if he gains the whole world and forfeits his soul?

JESUS IN MATTHEW 16:26

Most men pursue pleasure with such breathless haste that they hurry past it.

SØREN KIERKEGAARD

MY FIRST BOYFRIEND and I decided we could get married. Our make-out sessions communicated that we were destined at conception and pinnacled the night we dropped the L-bomb. Problem was (or problems were), we weren't right together long-term. On most occasions, we both knew it. We were on and off for a while, trying to convince ourselves that if we tried hard enough or prayed hard enough or thought hard enough, we could leap over any wall (see Psalm 18:29) and unfrustrate the issues frustrating our union. Eventually, we made a clean split and went our separate ways — not easily, mind you. It took me about as long as we'd dated to *actually* move on. Boyfriend #1 and I knew we *could* get married, united in values such as commitment and sacrifice and all those other sorts of marital verbiage. But we also realized that even though we *could*, the lack of our enduring peace shouted that we *shouldn't*.

While I was dining with friends recently, the evening's conversation turned to the topic of "choice," and I shared how there seems little incentive to commit these days: "If you don't like it, you're able to quit. If you don't like her, just break up — or transfer, or switch jobs, or leave that church, or move to another city." In other words, if something doesn't gel with *what you want*, there's bound to be a better option elsewhere, so why waste your time with any sort of commitment to a person, place, or even a belief?

I remember the crisp fall afternoon as if it were yesterday. With about a year's worth of following God under my belt, I was proudly divulging my newfound faith with a man I'd looked up to for a long time. Even as a less-than-religious teenager, I had always admired when this former coach would share his thoughts on marriage and its sacred dimensions. "Wait for it, Abbie. That's one of the best gifts you can offer God and yourself and the man you marry. Be patient and save yourself for the one," he'd say. Clearly at that stage in my life, theological reasoning wasn't compelling to me, but this man's pursuit of an idea worth living for, or waiting for, surely was. In a matter of moments though, his pedestal of commitment in my mind crumbled.

Giddily, I explained, "I understand now! And I agree with your thoughts on waiting and abstinence as something of great significance and even endearment."

He stared at me somewhat blankly and what seemed to be condescendingly.

"Oh, Abbie, college has you where it's meant to. I was like you for so long, too, thinking God must have a plan for my life and I was to wait for that *one*[1] special woman. But I guess something of a reality check hit me when I turned thirty." He continued, "I couldn't wait anymore, or maybe just didn't want to wait anymore. And God obviously didn't care about my desires or else He would've brought me a wife. So I finally gave up on Him and decided to face life's current situation by myself. God could tag along if He wanted, I guess, but life just seemed too short to keep playing the waiting game."

It was as though my nineteen-year-old passion had been squashed into the body of a nine-month-old who spilled her milk. I felt as though I'd done something frightfully wrong. It was as if I'd just shared the stupidest idea on earth. *But wait a minute*, I thought. *Wasn't this the man who'd initially drawn me toward the idea of saving sex until marriage?*

This crushed me on a number of fronts because it crushed my normal. And not only that, but it crushed the admired state my normal was striving for. C. S. Lewis said that reality is iconoclastic, meaning reality needs space to rebuild itself, continually refreshing its icons. The ways and wavelengths of reality get fuzzy, and lines get blurred over and tired of waiting, so we fall privy to creating our own.

My most forthright inner dialogues are usually about waiting for one thing or another, usually revolving around my anger that I have to keep waiting. And when I take it a step further, I realize that much of me prefers a fantasy. I'd rather have secure, easy, around-the-clock interaction with Eros than this vacancy. I want the honeymoon. I want feeling-based love and don't care if it's an illusion; even a temporary lure from the literal sounds lovely. I want lots of maids and margaritas and sex on warm sand. I want pleasure. I want flirting and feasts, with no morning after. Bottom line: Waiting is hard, and maintaining hope in the midst of waiting is harder, no matter how strong my beliefs. Waiting well, then, seems practically out of the question.

What would it look like to be content in our waiting and with our sexuality, as both singles and marrieds, not because we're perfect at waiting or sex or we're perfectly sexual but because we're content in our humanity, in our femininity and masculinity, in our longing for union with the Trinity? In *Earthen Vessels*, Matthew Anderson wrote,

Our union with Christ is the inauguration of a new form of life. When we hear and believe the good news that our sins have been washed away by the redemptive blood of Jesus Christ, the patterns and habits of our lives will never be left alone. That change in our status, wherein we transferred from the kingdom of darkness to the kingdom of God's glorious light, transforms our horizons and reorients our lives. Where our relationships were once marked by the hostility of violence, envy, pride, and anger, our union with Christ opens the possibility for a new mode of being.[2]

If we hope for freedom in our own physicality, we must be deeply aware of and appreciative of Jesus' physicality, or the physical nature of His incarnation and resurrection. Anderson goes on to write,

I am not my own. The body is for love and for God, not for my own pleasure and not for my own pain. The body is not for me, but for another. The kingdom is not for eating and drinking, but for righteousness, peace, and joy that come from living within the realm of love. God gives himself for us that we might give ourselves to him. And as hymn writer Robert Grant knew, the God who demonstrated His love for us by taking on a body and dying on a cross will be firm and faithful until the end:

Frail children of dust, and feeble as frail,

In thee do we trust, nor find thee to fail.

thy mercies how tender, how firm to the end!

our Maker, Defender, redeemer, and Friend.

This is the paradox of the body; the body is a temple, but the temple is in ruins. The incarnation of Jesus affirms the body's original goodness. The death of Jesus reminds us of its need for redemption. And the resurrection of Jesus gives us hope for its restoration.[3]

So much of waiting seems to be about trust, and so much of trust seems to be about waiting. It's easy to credit God when the wait sees pleasant results, but when He starts dishing out more waiting, or any amount of suffering, we start to question. We're not getting what we want, so we turn from God and take plans into our own hands, because in the words of Henri Nouwen, "It seems easier to be God than to love

God, easier to control people than to love people, easier to own life than to love life."[4]

Imagine being able to trust Jesus with your sexual desires. Imagine trusting that He's *actually* real and good and in control. Why wouldn't He care deeply about this massive part of your makeup that He made? Could believing such truths really boil down to trust, though? Furthermore, could the likes of your ability to wait, submit, lead, follow, be patient, like, love, discern, serve, listen, hear, worship, learn, keep the Sabbath, grow, follow, be humble, speak, be sexually healthy, or be lustfully holy all collide into the confines of this five-letter word?

As Dallas Willard put it,

> Jesus became flesh that he might redeem our bodies. Completions herein won't be completed until heaven, but even now, "if the Spirit of Him who raised Jesus from the dead dwells in you, He who raised Christ Jesus from the dead will also give life to your mortal bodies because of His Spirit who indwells you" (Romans 8:11). Our most radical response then is to "present our bodies as a living and holy sacrifice, very pleasing to God" (Romans 12:1-2, PAR). This total yielding of every part of our body to God, until the very tissues and muscles that make it up are inclined toward God and godliness and are vitalized in action by the powers of heaven, breaks all conformity with worldly life in this age and transforms us into conformity with the age to come, by completing the renewal of our minds — our powers of thought and imaginations and judgment, deeply rooted in our bodies. . . .
>
> There are no formulas — no definitive how-tos — for growth in the inner character of Jesus. Such growth is a way of relentless seeking. But there are many things we can do to place ourselves at the disposal of God, and "if with all our hearts we truly seek him, we shall surely find him" (Jeremiah 29:13, PAR). Or, as the prophet Azariah said, "If you seek Him, He will let you find Him" (2 Chronicles 15:2; see also 15:4).[5]

Women tend to settle, thinking, *What if no one else comes along?* while men tend to jump ship, thinking, *What if another comes along?*

There's a crowd of us who needs to lighten up at times, realizing casual dinner with someone of the opposite sex isn't going to kill us or cause us to settle eternally. But there's a larger crowd of us, I think, who needs to raise our standards and realize we have worth. Casual *anything* creates habituations. Noncommittal phrases such as "If I don't like him, we'll just break up" roll seamlessly into "If it doesn't work, we'll just get divorced." But settling isn't the core issue here; deficiency of our worth is.

We were made for more than we can now have or even have the capacity to have in our fallen nature. We were made for unblemished intimacy and the gourmet ecstasy. But we settle for crumbs. We settle for less because we're bored by waiting and discontent by our lot. Boredom says, "I'm unable to enjoy myself." Discontent says, "I should have become someone else by this point in my life." But what if God really knew what He was doing? And what if He didn't need our pending plans or stunted dreams to make His plans and dreams happen? What if Love really never ended or failed (see 1 Corinthians 13:8) and truly came first (see 1 John 4:19) and followed after (see Exodus 14:19)? What if He truly was quick to forgive and quicker to unleash mercy (see Joel 2:13)? What if Love's ways were always creating (see Genesis 1:1), restoring, and searching for ways to capture us anew (see Psalm 139:23), especially that which feels dead and broken (see Ezekiel 37:1-14)? What if God knew what He was doing, even in the midst of suffering (see Job 30:26-27; Isaiah 53:3; Romans 5:3)? And what if He was at work precisely in our silent caverns of waiting?

FOR FURTHER MUSING AND DISCUSSION

1. What are your earliest memories of hearing about sex or abstinence? Did you think sex was bad or good? Who shared this information with you, and what did you think of that person?

2. How have your early views about sex shifted since your childhood? (Maybe sketching a timeline would be helpful here, with notches at five years old, ten, fifteen, twenty, etc.)

3. Whether it relates to sex, getting married, or being a mother, what's most challenging for you about the process of waiting?

Too Dirty for Grace[1]

She lives for the sake of the body,
Loves for the life of her enemy,
Gives to the needs of her neighbor,
Serves for the kingdom of Christ.
And she has chlamydia.

*Is this disease a part of me, or is it a product of my whole? Am
I still part of the body, or must the body part with my soul?*

She evangelizes others' senses,
Hoping to numb her own,
Giving herself away,
At the cost of losing her way,
from Worth, Dignity, and Beauty,
Identity, Security, and Purity.

*Is my body diseased, or is it the fulfillment of me? Am I too
dirty for Grace, or Grace too disgraced by this she?*

Feeling dirty and ashamed,
Unworthy and untamed,
Forsaken from her true Love,
She cries herself to sleep.

*How could I be so wretched? How could I be such a fool? I
want to lose this addiction, to silence its whispering rules.
Come near to me, my Jesus. Come near and make me clean.
Come near to my desperate longings, longings to be Naked
and Seen. I want to love and serve and give to You alone; I
want to live and breathe and believe as if I'm Your own. Remind
me that I am clean; tell my body that she is Yours; whisper
Truths to my new creation; teach me that I am adored.*

CHAPTER 11

BROKENNESS AND LUST

The heart has its reasons, which reason does not know. We feel it in a thousand things. It is the heart which experiences God, and not the reason. This, then, is faith: God felt by the heart, not by the reason.

BLAISE PASCAL

Desire is the path to experiencing God. Desire in all its forms. Even our dark desires, the ones we're most fearful and ashamed of, the ones we call sin. Even those desires are merely disfigured drives searching for the divine in counterfeit form — original desires leading toward Home.

SHANE HIPP, *Flickering Pixels*

All things were made through him, and without him was not any thing made that was made. In him was life, and the life was the light of men. The light shines in the darkness, and the darkness has not overcome it.

JOHN 1:3-5

I USED TO wonder if being single was a product of the Fall. Then I started wondering beyond consequences, into sensations. Like how did falling feel when Eve consciously chose to do what she'd been told not to by God (see Genesis 2:25–3:7)? How did it taste to bite into something that changed everything? What was the smell when a new consciousness covered the soul of humanity, stealing innocence and leaving behind shame, tagging sin into our deepest parts (most destructively, maybe, the part of sexuality)? Was everything still and silent, all of life wholly organic and real, a holy reality, until the fruit's skin was punctured? What did it sound like and look like? Did Eve's appearance change when death was born? Did Adam scream at his lover's choice, or creation at these lovers' grandiose illusions?

It may be too simplistic to say that anything *of God* is real and anything *not of God* is unreal (or sin). But I think it's at least fair to say that *reality* is rooted in the Garden of Eden, whereas *unreality* is the unrooted stem that launches so many of our fictitious quests. It tempts our palates to satisfactions *other* than God so that *just God* no longer satisfies (see Ecclesiastes 1:8; Haggai 1:6; Hebrews 3:8-11). "Surely you want more, surely you need the forbidden," the serpent tells us, "to become most like your Maker" (see Genesis 3:4-5). Because of the Fall, what is actually real now feels far-fetched. And what is actually an illusion seems a worthwhile reality—especially for us churchy folks, I think. "Friendships" on Facebook, chat rooms, or pornography (and the list could go on) often feel more preferable to us than that which is true and just and truly loving: intimacy. I'm thankful God has never been surprised by such twisted realities or overwhelmed by our fantasies and erroneous thinking. He's never been caught off guard by our choices, calloused by our pain, or corroded by our persistent pleas. He knows exactly where we are at all times; He follows our thought trails and chooses to stay. Yet He's the unconditional love I consistently resist—the transcendent lover from whom I'm prone to wander. Why? Because although I'm saved, or justified, by my faith in Jesus Christ, I'm still being sanctified, or made new, every passing moment.

In *Community and Growth*, Jean Vanier wrote,

> To welcome is to be open to reality as it is, with the least possible filtering. I have discovered that I have many filters within my own self where I select and modify the reality I want to welcome: the reality of the world, of people,

of God and of the Word of God. I select what pleases me, boosts my ego and gives me a sense of worth. I reject that which causes inner pain or disturbance or a feeling of helplessness; that which may bring up guilt feelings or anger or a broken sexuality. We all have filters created from our early childhood, protecting our vulnerable hearts and minds. To grow is to let go of these filters and to welcome the reality that is given, no longer through preconceived ideas, theories, prejudgements or prejudices or through our wounded emotions, but just as it is. Thus, we are in truth and no longer in a world of illusions.[2]

Brokenness comes with the package of a beating heart and breathing lungs. Whether manifested through a broken heart, body, spirit, or mind, brokenness is a part of being human. Yet we run from it. We treat it like a cancer, like a part of us that is wrong and needs to be defeated, like an obstacle preventing our wholeness. Every once in a while, we come across people willing to work with their brokenness versus fighting it and we sense that they're refreshing to be around. There's something real about brokenness, something authentic and genuine. It's a window, of sorts, to seeing what is whole.

None of us escapes addiction. And though some addictions are more identifiable (porn, food, shopping), others (self-promotion, comfort, vanity) are heinously scripted into our DNA. Today, my friend told me she was an addict. I was so proud of her, not because she confessed some profane form of activity but because she cooperated with some unpleasant part of being human. My friend and I realized that to sever her addiction altogether would mean severing parts of her that were good, like desire. Yet fully submitting to its patterns felt excruciating as well, so we decided there must be an alternative route.

Maybe recovery is less about learning how not to fall than about recognizing tools to help us get back up, and maybe strands of addiction will always taunt us. But healing is less about being fixed than about being loved, especially in our addictions. We can either turn away from our addictions or face the truth of them and fix our eyes on the Truth of Love in that vicinity (see Psalm 119:15; Hebrews 12:2). In the words of Jean Vanier,

> We are all handicapped before God, prisoners of our own egoism. But Jesus has come to heal us, save us and set us free by the gift of His Spirit. That is the good news He brings to the poor: we are not alone in our sadness, darkness and loneliness, in our fears and emotional and sexual problems. He loves us and is with us: "Do not be afraid, I am with you."[3]

Men are often accused as the lustful, gluttonous whores of anything sexual, but women can struggle here as well.[4] I promise. We may be less apt to look at naked males (or maybe not) or bring up a conversation about masturbation, but we'll gladly worship page after page of airbrushed images or eye every curve of any female in our midst. We lust after what each other has, arousing envy and massaging covet deep into our beings. If a guy reaches the kind of high-pitched libido that foreplay raises, he'll want more and often push for it. Women can wear this jewelry of persuasion too; it just sparkles differently. We wave the wand of seduction (a sick twist on sexuality) to get what we want, when we want it. Feminine charm reels guys in, grabs what it wants, and then leaves the guy reeling, all because we didn't want to wait or we didn't get what we wanted in the waiting zone. And for neither of us is this based on our being lustful, gluttonous whores; rather, it's based on our being humans, in need of a Savior. A girl may question how one could ponder sex every 3.5 minutes, until she's lent the comparison of how often she ponders food, weight, and body insecurity. What started out as two bites of dessert can end up leaving two empty boxes (plus an empty ice cream container), and this can occur just as voraciously as a tiny-teed waitress can lead a guy into a night of fantasy and screen-enabled sex. All of this to say, the speed and ways at which humanity can turn selfward holds no gender partiality. We *all* need help.

There are days when I feel as though I understand pornography and sex-related addictions, and there are days when I don't. Last night was one of the don'ts. I walked into a video store, and while I was checking out, a slightly rushed gentleman walked past me toward a door marked "Adults Only," which had gone unnoticed to me until that point.

"Sir, I need to see your ID," the young clerk said.

"I'm in here all the time," the man responded. "Why do you always have to ask?"

"It's policy, sir."

He showed the clerk his card, never making eye contact with me, and proceeded through the white door. Feeling naive and taken aback, I proceeded with my checkout. The clerk didn't say anything, but his eyes told me he was sorry. He seemed to hate seeing this as much as I did.

Most of what I recall from last night is the man's face, frustrated and anxious, and the gold band around his ring finger. What gives the footage behind that door such a strong grip? What is this man's thought process, and what is he actually wanting? Is it connection, intimacy, or maybe an expression of relief? Clearly, I didn't know him, but what is the most beneficial thing even to pray at this point? Or when I do cross paths with someone I know in this scenario, what is most helpful to say? What does he need to hear? What is her heart craving? Am I willing to let such brokenness and twisted sexuality exist in my circle of acquaintance? Furthermore, am I willing to believe that God's love can exist in such twistedness?

What if we remembered that every person we crossed paths with today had some level of brokenness? And what if that brokenness was the window to seeing what is whole?

The man at the counter.

The woman at the gas station.

The driver you flipped off en route to work.

The waiter at the Mexican restaurant.

The pregnant lady at the pool.

The actor.

The trucker.

The doctor.

The pastor.

The student.

The mom.

The boy laughing.

The woman crying.

The man praying.

The child.

They're just like the rest of us; we're just like them. As Larry Crabb explains,

The good in every Christian's soul waiting to be released beneath all the emotional and selfish rubble is the longing to be relationally holy, the urge to bless, to turn the other cheek, to live responsibly, to suffer well, to hope, to rejoice during hard times. And that set of urges, which controlled every moment of Jesus' life on earth, has been given to us in the gospel.[5]

The following conversation transpired with a college student recently:

"So, what's going on with you spiritually?" I asked through the steam of two cups of coffee.

"You know, I'm doing okay but really struggling in a certain area."

"Hmmm," I said, quite certain I knew where we were heading. "Would you feel comfortable unpacking the struggle a little more?"

"Yeah, I guess . . . I mean, I think a lot of people struggle with it too. It's just that, well, I don't really know what to do about it. Like, I don't really know why it's been so bad lately."

"Well," I said, seeing shame embodied before me, "let's try to at least get this 'it' on the table, and then maybe we'll go from there."

"Okay . . . well, it's just this problem with . . . lust. I think about the opposite sex and sex and just lustful stuff all the time."

"Okay," I said, "talk to me about those thoughts a little more."

"Um, I don't know what else to say. It's just really bad and really gross."

At this point, the student became more frustrated at the "it," or the self, or something of the two. "It's like I can't get lustful thoughts out of my head. And they come up at random times, like while I'm trying to study or watch TV or even trying to pray!"

"Seems that God is unveiling a lot here. Thank you for being willing to talk about it. It's clearly been burdening you a lot."

"Yeah . . . yeah, it really has," the student said, looking down at the table. "I hate it. And I hate me when I hate it. And I can't imagine how God would want anything to do with this—and definitely me in this."

How does lust carry such power in our Christian lives and such persistence in our Christian journeys? How does something so good and potentially full of opportunity become such an evil in an untraceable matter of seconds? The etymology of *lust* exposes original uses of "joyful and merry" and, some years later, "full of healthy vigor." Christian interpretation introduced lust's negative lens. *Easton's 1897 Bible Dictionary* explained it in two ways: sinful longings (see Romans 1:21 [the inward sin that leads to the falling away from God]) and objects of desire (see Mark 4:19). Apparently, lust, then, must not *always* be tagged as "sin," must not always be branded as bad. Furthermore, what if this four-letter word had boastful potentials of vigor for Jesus, with plausible gain, not guilt? What if lust could be a gift?

I once heard it said that finding the humility and strength to take God into our lust would free us from the sins of lust.[6] In other words, while in the pursuit of God, even lust—something typically assumed as unquestionably and utterly disgusting—has the potential to be offered as a means of holiness. Even lust has the grace-drenched capacity to be used for something good. If God is good and at work in all things, at all times, then with lust, too, there must be a redeeming perspective. In Christ, even lust may be used as a gateway into sanctification and glorifying God.

Lust itself, then, is not our ultimate problem nor its absence our solution. Lust is a product of the Fall and of being a member of a fallen race. So is lust sin? Or equal in weight to sins of jealousy or laziness, curiosity or telling a white lie (which is a lie, by the way)? Well, yes, in the sense that we are born into sin (see Psalm 51:5) and that no good thing exists apart from the Father (see Psalm 14:1; 53:1; Mark 10:18), making *all things* laden with sin, apart from His hand, including lust (among the others). We are soaked from the start in an oceanic proclivity *against* our Maker, and only by being made new (see 2 Corinthians 5:17) and reborn in the Spirit of Christ do we have the opportunity to tether our days, and lusts, to the Godhead. To *relearn love* is a lifelong process of tethering our affections to the One for whom they were originally and most fully intended.

We are born sexual because we are born human. To have sexual energy is a given when we're talking about males and females. It's not a curse or precursor to evil but rather a product of being human and made in God's image. The most fully human person to ever walk this earth was Jesus. He had hormones and a sex drive and experienced every temptation I have (see Hebrews 4:15) but never had sex and never sinned. When I feel Jesus is too clean to engage with my messiness or I am too dirty to interact with His holiness, He's not the Lover I was made for, nor is my trust in my needed Savior. The question is, do I believe this?

FOR FURTHER MUSING AND DISCUSSION

1. What does this chapter communicate about brokenness? Is that how you tend to view it, or is brokenness something you tend to resist, ignore, or deny altogether?
2. How has pornography affected your life?
3. Have you ever known someone with lust, or great vigor and passion, for God? What's it like being around that person?
4. What does it mean to you that Jesus was the most fully human person to ever walk this earth?

Part of me loves and respects men so desperately, and part of me thinks they are so embarrassingly incompetent at life and in love. You have to teach them the very basics of emotional literacy. You have to teach them how to be there for you, and part of me feels tender toward them and gentle, and part of me is so afraid of them, afraid of any more violation.

ANNE LAMOTT, *Operating Instructions:*
A Journal of My Son's First Year

CHAPTER 12

SEX

Almost all Americans have sex before marrying, according to premarital sex research that shows such behavior is the norm in the U.S. and has been for the past 50 years. The new study shows that by age 20, 75% of Americans have had premarital sex. That number rises to 95% by age 44.

WEBMD.COM

Sex is, in Paul's image, a joining of your body to someone else's. In baptism, you have become Christ's body, and it is Christ's body that must give you permission to join his body to another body. In the Christian grammar, we have no right to sex. The place where the Church confers that privilege on you is the wedding. . . . Chastity, in other words, is a fact of gospel life. In the New Testament, sex beyond the boundaries of marriage — the boundaries of communally granted sanction of sex — is simply off limits. . . . Abstinence before marriage, and fidelity within marriage; any other kind of sex is embodied apostasy.

LAUREN WINNER, *Real Sex*

MOST OF MY single friends have lost their virginity — some in ways that are devastating and some in ways that are enviable. The extent to which sex is "sleeping around" in today's culture is beyond measure. On a daily basis, most of us are sold endless (semi-enticing) reasons not to wait. When I was in middle school, "BJs" were the big deal. Getting there was like getting to home base. Middle schoolers today have told me that oral sex is expected and that intercourse is the only real home run. People have always shacked up prior to the altar, but "religious people," at least, haven't always taken quite the ease (at least publicly) in doing so as our generation. According to research, "Among women ages eighteen to twenty-three currently in nonmarital relationships, only 4 percent are not sexually involved with their partner. (The figure for noninvolvement is slightly higher for men because fewer men consider their sexual attachments to be relationships.)"[1]

In David Kinnaman's *You Lost Me*, he said,

> Young Christians' church experiences related to sexuality are often simplistic, judgmental. With unfettered access to digital pornography and immersed in a culture that values hyper-sexuality over wholeness, teen and twenty-something Christians are struggling with how to live meaningful lives in terms of sex and sexuality. One of the significant tensions for many young believers is how to live up to the church's expectations of chastity and sexual purity in this culture, especially as the age of first marriage is now commonly delayed to the late twenties. Research indicates that most young Christians are as sexually active as their non-Christian peers, even though they are more conservative in their attitudes about sexuality. One-sixth of young Christians (17%) said they "have made mistakes and feel judged in church because of them."[2]

Sex is arguably our greatest gift and most fragile jewel. It'll fight any competitor on earth and usually win. And whether under the garments of a happily married couple or the sheets of a single teen, it's a pleasure key that can unlock and answer most doors. But it can lock and shut them just as quickly. Especially in the church, questions like "How far is too far?" and "How far can we go before we've gone too far?" have dominated for a long time. And, unfortunately, they've left few answers offering little more than tasteless blends of unmet fear and guilt, making me think there must be more important, or expansive, questions we're overlooking.

It took me reading through Song of Solomon's love poems to

realize that God wasn't quite as pent up and ashamed of sex as I tended to be. Yet it was also evident that He was distinct in ordering its time and placement. A healthy engagement with our singleness requires a healthy engagement with our sexuality. Sexuality is part of our humanity, and without it, we're incomplete. If at some point we get engaged, we Christians tend to feel liberated to enter the "sex conversations," but before that it's too often (explicitly and implicitly) considered taboo and out of God's comfort zone. Rechanneling our interiorities, however, necessitates a willingness to ask hard questions and question hard answers, trusting that the God who made us is willing to be there with us, even when we feel trashy or R-rated (see Isaiah 41:9-10). There are no new thoughts under the sun (see Ecclesiastes 1:9), but there are also no thoughts too absurd, or unkempt, for new exploration.

Dallas Willard explains,

> For good or for evil the body lies right at the center of the spiritual life — a strange combination of words to most people. One can immediately see all around us that the human body is a (perhaps in some cases even the) primary barrier to conformity to Christ. But this certainly was not God's intent for the body. It is not in the nature of the body as such. (The body is not inherently evil.) Nor is it even caused by the body. But still it is a fact that the body usually hinders people in doing what they know to be good and right. Being formed in evil it, in turn, fosters evil and constantly runs ahead of our good intentions — but in the opposite direction.
>
> Still, our body is a good thing. God made it for good. That is why Jesus Christ is so relentlessly incarnational. The body should be cherished and properly cared for, not as our master, however, but as a servant of God. For most people, on the other hand, their body governs their life. And that is the problem. Even professing Christians, by and large, devote to their spiritual growth and well-being a tiny fraction of the time they devote to their body, and it is an even tinier fraction if we include what they worry about.[3]

My older sister was the first person to tell me about sex. I grew up thinking girls were good and boys had cooties, marriage was good and sex was gross. But when I was about thirteen, my sister divulged to me a whole new set of views on girls, boys, marriage, and sex, and they were all piled into the same multifaceted box. My first french kiss was at fifteen. I couldn't have cared less about God at that point and simply wanted to be sought after by my pubescent counterpart, yet when we started kissing, I abruptly stopped, pulled back, and said, "We can't have sex! We can't have sex!" I wasn't afraid of sex, I don't think, but deep down I knew that something about it seemed premature prior to marriage. Even as a teenager, far removed from knowing or caring about Jesus, I had a convicted desire to preserve some aspect of sex. I had a deep-seated belief that God's intentions for sexual relations were reserved for marriage.

It's thoughtful of God to wire our bodies for sexual union and to wire all things sexual (a kiss, a caress, lovers hand in hand) toward an end of sex, but it's challenging for us non-hitcheds that sex was designed for a prescribed environment. Although forgivable when misplaced (see Psalm 130:3-4; Colossians 2:13; Romans 8:1), sex is intended for the context of marriage (see Mark 10:8; Hebrews 13:4). And though all of us are well aware of various ways to get around this prescription, the original (and, thus, most glorifying, satisfying, and pleasurable) order cannot be undone, nor can we turn from it without consequence. Sex in the context of marriage is of the most miraculous and mysterious designs, and sex outside of marriage is arguably of the most destructive perversions from the original design:

> Though our sexuality is created as God's perfect design, we are also excruciatingly aware of the distortions that have occurred through the consequences of sin, fallen nature and deviation from God's original design. This good gift of sex has been perverted and corrupted in our secular world, which is why it is such a struggle for most people. Inauthentic sexuality, a consequence of our fallen condition, leaves us open to unreal, false, convoluted and unreliable messages about sexuality and sexual behaviors. This

happens through the interplay of societal attitudes and beliefs, sociocultural structures, biological and psychological factors, as well as individual choice and human agency. In short, authentic sexuality has to do with human beings seeking to live as sexual beings according to God's design and purpose. . . .

Because procreation is not the exclusive reason for sexual expression, sexual desire and fulfillment between man and woman have divine meaning and purpose as well. . . .[4]

Our disturbed sexual natures are only one aspect of a disturbed and abnormal universe. Our understanding of this ought to keep us from overrating the seriousness of our sexual struggles. We should be no more surprised by the constancy and diversity of our sexual struggles than we are by our moral struggles regarding work, money, possessions, family obligations, or anything else that the Ten Commandments highlight as areas of life in special need of regulation.[5]

I've never met a married person who wished he'd had premarital sex or who regretted that she didn't. And I've talked to thousands who, when given the hypothetical chance to take back any experience, name one of sexual nature. For marrieds, sex is to be viewed and treated as the gift it was prescribed to be. And for singles, sex is to be viewed and treated as the gift it was prescribed to be. And for both, consequences (namely, guilt and shame) will arise when treated otherwise.

Sex before marriage is misplaced—out of bounds from its intended position (and, thus, potential). So by toying around with its out-of-bounds areas, I'm not only teasing myself and another but cheating myself and another from the climactic field for which sex—and its participants—was intended. I've learned this the hard way. Though still a virgin, I've danced close enough to sexual lines to know that, yes, premarital sexual energy may provide momentary pleasure, but, no, it does nothing beneficial for the long term and, in fact, does quite the opposite. I've found it to confuse intimacy and condemn, to build up self-hatred and tear down respect, both for myself and for the person I'm messing around with.

Biblical times had a lot less premarital sex happening because folks married at far younger ages. Most sex, then, was happening *after* someone was married, either with his spouse, which was good, or with someone else, which was prohibited. That may explain why the Scriptures focus a lot more on adultery than premarital sex. Hebrews 13:4 mentions two types of prohibited sex: *moichos*, which refers to a married person having sex with someone other than his or her spouse (adultery), and *porneia*, referencing any other unmarried sex, most commonly translated as fornication or sexual immorality (the root semantic is unsurprising here: "porn"). First Corinthians 6:12-20 tells us to "flee" from this (*porneia*) because the body is the temple of the Holy Spirit and we are to honor God with our bodies. Paul was thought to be referencing morality and personal purity here. In the original Greek, however, *you* is plural and *body* is singular, so it's likely that Paul was also making reference to the church — the bride of Christ. First Thessalonians 4:3-5 calls us to avoid *porneia* and learn to "abstain from sexual immorality; that each one of you know how to control his own body in holiness and honor, not in the passion of lust like the Gentiles who do not know God." If you're still not convinced of sexual danger or God's high treatment of its domain, read Exodus, Deuteronomy, and Leviticus.

Bottom line: We are born sexual. Our bodies are mysteriously and naturally inclined toward sex, even the devoutly Christian body. And uncontained, sex can be disastrous. Not unlike uncontained fire, sex apart from a monogamous marital status can wreak havoc beyond words. And particularly when the couple is "in love" and longing for nothing more than "making love," resisting sexual aspects of love is difficult. I am convinced that man and woman cannot resist sexual temptation without similarly resisting realities of their humanity. Hope for sexual purity must lie in a pure and undefiled openness to one's worth before God, as well as a recognition of one's fallenness and need for His ongoing saving grace. Even then, it will be a fight.

My counsel to those who are unmarried and sleeping together is to legitimize it and get married or stop sleeping together. If you're not ready to do either, take this as you will, but you'd be wise to take some time apart. God will be gracious enough to let you do it your way, but from everything I've ever seen and heard, I can promise you in confidence that His way will have a better outcome for you and your guy or gal friend.

Whether a person is single, dating, engaged, or married, the biblical message is markedly clear: Sex outside marriage is a perversion of the intended design and is bound for unpleasant consequences, if not now, soon. Wherever these pages find you, keep in mind that holiness is about identity, not morality. We don't become holy by attaining a level of holiness or abstaining from the unholiness of something sexual; we are holy because we are called holy by Holiness Himself. Holiness hides in us. Our holiness is hidden in Christ. We are fallen and picked up by Holiness. We are twisted, and we are holy because of God.

FOR FURTHER MUSING AND DISCUSSION

1. Why do you think God cares about sex so much?
2. Spend some time pondering this quote:

> I've never met a married person who wished he'd had premarital sex or who regretted that she didn't. And I've talked to thousands who, when given the hypothetical chance to take back any experience, name one of sexual nature. For marrieds, sex is to be viewed and treated as the gift it was prescribed to be. And for singles, sex is to be viewed and treated as the gift it was prescribed to be. And for both, consequences (namely, guilt and shame) will arise when treated otherwise.

Do you relate? Agree? Disagree?

Simon

What did it feel like?

What did he feel like?

Why him in the first place?

Why not others on the road?

Did they yell at him or beat him?

Did he fight back?

How much force did agreement take?

How much weight did agreement bear?

Did he know the cause, or cost, at hand? Or its effect?

Did he even know who Jesus was?

How long was the walk?

How long till he heard the whole story?

Did he need to hear the whole story?

What does it mean that Sovereignty allows crosses?

Allows us to carry crosses?

Chooses us to carry crosses?

And sometimes forces us to?

What would it look like to engage with this scene — with our own crosses, good and bad, chosen and forced, called for and for which we've been called?

"As they went out, they found a man of Cyrene, Simon by name. They compelled this man to carry his cross" (Matthew 27:32).

CHAPTER 13

BOUNDARIES

Modesty is the proof that morality is sexy. It may even be the proof of God, because it means that we have been designed in such a way that when we humans act like animals, without any restraint and without any rules, we just don't have as much fun.

WENDY SHALIT

We are half-hearted creatures, fooling about with drink and sex and ambition when infinite joy is offered us, like an ignorant child who wants to go on making mud pies in a slum because he cannot imagine what is meant by the offer of a holiday at the sea. We are far too easily pleased.

C. S. LEWIS

I WAS ASKING an African friend lately why shorts were such a no-go in many countries there or why long skirts are considered more appropriate than pants. She explained that unlike America, "breasts aren't anything special in my land. Women whip them out to feed, just like they'd whip out a bottle, or a tube of lipstick. But thighs," she explained, "are the novelty. They're the breasts of the West."

Clearly, cultures differ on views of kissing, caressing, masturbating, dating, dancing, finances, chivalry, and drinking, as do denominations, generations, and geographic locations. Wearing a two-piece swimsuit in southern California may go without question, but if you so much as show a midriff line in some other circles, you're fired or will burn in the fires of hell. Some cultures date one way, while others do so entirely differently. What's "right" for you may be "wrong" for them, or at least not practiced. How do we assemble answers, then, or at least similar responses? I think part of it narrows down to something about love and surrender. When my being right trumps my willingness to love, or my way trumps my compassion, I've lost the True path.

Jesus said He came that we may have life and have it abundantly (see John 10:10), but I often wonder what that's got to do with the limits of life. When a four-year-old recently asked me why he couldn't play with the boiling water, I remembered that boundaries are good and, in fact, make space for abundance. Boundaries tell where one is and how much space she has to roam. They provide safety, bearings, and an awareness of where one is. Boundaries are good and God-given but hard to accept. When I taste good chocolate, the last thing I want to do is stop at the boundary of one serving (or one bar!). And pertaining to sex, when my senses are aroused by anything halfway sexual, I want the whole.

To me, sex is sex—whether anal, oral, or genital—and as discussed previously, I do not believe it was intended outside of marriage. Furthermore, I believe physical interactions should stop at a point that loses, or even limits, the edification of the Body of Christ. A simple way of defining this personally has been questioning what I would feel comfortable doing in a public setting. In other words, my whole life yearns to be a reflection of and offer an invitation into the gospel of Jesus Christ. Even in expressions of my sexuality and sexual interactions, my hope is to remember that although I may feel alone with one other person, I am still attached to a bigger set of persons called the Body of Christ.

Our bodies are the temple of the Holy Spirit, who is in us, whom we have received from God, joined to Christ Himself (see 1 Corinthians 6:19-20). In Paul's words, the body is not meant for immorality but for the Lord, and the Lord for the body (see 1 Corinthians 6:13-16). The

Spirit transforms and enables us toward the fullness of our bodily humanity and the respected humanity of others. Moving toward God in relationship means moving toward purity, self-control, and mutual honor of one another's bodies, resisting impulses of possession and lust for personal gain.

In *Celebrating the Single Life*, Susan Muto said,

> Faith, hope and self-giving love are essential to the single life. Only to the degree that we acknowledge our being cared for by God can we experience each other as *Thou* and never as *It*. For this reason many single persons realize that casual, self-indulging sexuality can never make one happy. To treat the other as an object of genital gratification leaves one feeling harsh, empty and sadly unfulfilled. Real love can best be experienced between single persons when they reverence one another's integrity in God.[1]

She went on to say in a later chapter,

> Thus, we are called to set high standards that exemplify the art of loving. This means rising above the tendency not to get involved with others and truly befriending them. Such loving includes the risk of falling into emotional exclusiveness and consequent envy and jealousy. It also includes the risk of betrayed trust, mutual strife and power struggles. But what is the alternative? A selfish, little life, isolated and withdrawn, that casts a shadow over the single vocation as such. Too often single persons end up without any friends because they fear the risk of loving. . . .
>
> As a single person, He [Jesus] had about Him an ease, graciousness and affection that could draw all hearts. He touched responsive chords in whoever met Him, sharing with them wonder and joy as well as grief and weariness. He could thrill to the appeal of nature and be delighted by the innocence of a child. As witnesses to the art of Christlike loving, we must not reduce singleness to some type of disembodied existence. We love as full-blooded, enfleshed men and women who run the risk of loving as Christ did.[2]

It's commonplace to hear statements like "As long as I'm not hurting people, what I do with my body is my business. And, anyway, it's not like what I do in my bedroom affects the one next door!" I disagree. To me, anything related to our humanity, including our sexuality, is sacred and is never to be left in secret nor understood apart from our existence. Humanity and sexuality aren't exclusive—highly personal, maybe, but not private. As Archbishop Desmond Tutu said,

> We think of ourselves far too frequently as just individuals, separated from one another, whereas you are connected and what you do affects the whole world. When you do well, it spreads out; it is for the whole of humanity. Ubuntu[3] is the essence of being a person. It means that we are people through other people. We cannot be fully human alone. We are made for interdependence; we are made for family. When you have ubuntu, you embrace others. You are generous, compassionate. If the world had more ubuntu, we would not have war. We would not have this huge gap between the rich and the poor. You are rich so that you can make up what is lacking for others. You are powerful so that you can help the weak, just as a mother or father helps their children. This is God's dream.[4]

God is one, but God is also submissive to the communal. And He invites us to be His community. We are wired to affect one another; if I am in true relationship with you, my stuff reaches into your stuff, and my issues are more rightfully understood in engagement with the companionship of yours. Private, personal issues seem far less scary when they've come out, when they've gone public. What if marrieds talked to singles about the joys of committed sex, and singles to marrieds about the dilemmas of sought-after chastity? What if we knew what we were doing was affecting those around us and viewed that as an opportunity eliciting safety, confession, and repentance, not condemnation and shame?

But what about friendships with the opposite sex? Is there such a thing as platonic, and should boundaries be involved? It *seems* that guy/girl friendships should give you the best of both worlds; you get to be flirty and flamboyant but avoid risk and heartbreak. The reality is that guy/girl friendships can often be the most trying and painful because they're emotionally penetrating. We can cake ourselves so committedly with purity and physical self-control that we figure a little emotional icing won't harm the halo. Whether it's talking on the phone till wee hours or sharing meals five times a week, often we find ourselves emotionally dating someone, but doing so without a second thought because "we don't really like him; he's just a friend!"[5] However, intimacy without commitment can too easily cause bitterness and eventual hatred.[6]

Two single buddies and I downloaded our needy souls for a handful of hours recently in the Carl's Jr. parking lot. We stripped down to bare emotions and expected no fumble. One of the friends said afterward, "We just committed relational suicide." What he meant was that the levels of intimacy we'd unveiled have little to no beneficial value. Vulnerability without safety is destructive. And emotional chastity is just as valuable as physical. It's my heart that's called the wellspring of life (see Proverbs 4:23), not my hymen. A shared part of my heart is a shared part of me, never to be unshared. It's a delicate vessel worthy of giving, for sure, but also of delicate guarding.

Am I saying group dating is bad or that one-on-one time with friends of the opposite sex is wrong? I'll lend such severity to neither, but for me personally, female friends are my closest. I certainly don't avoid male friendships, but I also don't prioritize them. If I (or they) marry someday, the relationship is bound to shift and, thus, it's better to invest in secure, lasting friendships than set myself (and another) up for deeper grief and loss than necessary.

/ / / / /

Our bodies are not evil. Jesus Himself came in bodily form. Untethered to its Artist, however, the body is unable to remember its true state of communion and will remain in a perpetual search for freedom and true relationship. Bodies are the vessel by which we live, move, and breathe. They were made for relationship with God and others. The first human relationship started with a bodily connection. Eve came from Adam's body. Furthermore, our bodies, as well as Adam's and Eve's, were made to be touched. And made to interact and connect. Our bodies were made sexual. And through His Son, by His Spirit, as His bridegroom, our bodies were made for committed, intimate union with God. All sounds lovely for the married crowd among us, eh? What if you were to reread the last paragraph and realize it is true for the single crowd as well?

In her book *Unsqueezed*, Margot Starbuck lists aspects of the body and what they are meant to do: work, bless, serve, create, build, love, pray, play, worship, and procreate.[7] First of all, notice that the only separation point for us as singles is procreation. Second, notice the amount of freedom these words represent. Notice how they affect you compared to this list: rules, no, stop, don't, fix, tear down. Some Christians talk a lot about what we're *not to do*. But what if we disbanded the curses of condemnation we've put on ourselves, unloosed our hands from around our necks, and started to live and move and breathe again.

Some people like to quote Proverbs 4:23 about guarding our hearts,[8] and when doing so, we tend to misinterpret the passage as being about denying our hearts or self-protecting. Indirectly, we say, "Stuff your feelings and ignore the reality of what's going on in you. The heart is deceitful above all things" (see Jeremiah 17:9). What if Jeremiah's meaning here was less about the heart being evil and more about it having a mind of its own and, thus, an ability to win us over or deceive our processing at any given moment? What if the redeemed heart was found complex and complicated but not *bad*? And what if we realized that each of us has different physical, emotional, and spiritual needs and that refreshment and healing to one soul may mean starvation to another? Guarding our hearts, then, would be based on knowing our hearts (expectations, limitations, desires, hesitations, scars) and learning our hearts' healthy fences rather than shutting off or detaching from them altogether.[9] Hearts, feelings, desires, longings, and lusts should not be our end-all compass, but they are made in God's image too (see Genesis 1:26), not as stable leaders but as exposing windows into our souls. When we discover our heart's worth and, therefore, *our* worth, because of who we are in Christ, we discover the gift of our hearts, a tool by which God communicates:

> We must maintain a holy jealousy of ourselves, and set a strict guard, accordingly, upon all the avenues of the soul; keep our hearts from doing hurt and getting hurt, from being defiled by sin and disturbed by trouble; keep them as our jewel, as our vineyard; keep a conscience void of offence; keep out bad thoughts; keep the affections upon right objects and in due bounds. Keep them with all keepings (so the word is); there are many ways of keeping things — by care, by strength, by calling in help, and we must use them all in keeping our hearts.[10]

I've watched dating couples abstain from everything surrounding touch and seen their relationship get pretty messed up. And I've watched couples practice healthy touch and seen it to be highly beneficial. In other words, there are more paths to purity than merely avoiding touch. If you can't date without physicality, what happens if you marry and due to paralyzation or disease lose the ability to be physically intimate with your spouse? So maybe sex or no sex isn't the primary topic we should be discussing. Maybe inner virginity and purity and purification are as concerning to God as outer behaviors. And maybe God really is for me, not against me (see Romans 8:31), so that what I do doesn't necessarily change His views of me but elicits His hurt for me.

My immodesty doesn't make God stumble, but it saddens Him because it reflects my stumbling esteem. He is heartbroken when I am heartbroken and hates when I am hating myself. Waiting for church-sanctioned sex, then, isn't just because God said so (see Acts 15:20; 1 Corinthians 5:1; 6:13,18; 7:2; 10:8; Galatians 5:19; Ephesians 5:3; Colossians 3:5; 1 Thessalonians 4:3; Jude 1:7; Hebrews 13:4) but because I have an inner peace affirming this resolve. My desire to be holy is in part because God is holy (see Exodus 3:5; Leviticus 19:2; Psalm 30:4; 1 Peter 1:16 [there are literally hundreds of references here]) but also because I was made to be holy (see Ezekiel 20:41; John 14; 2 Thessalonians 1:10-12), and in pursuing holiness, I find myself most alive. Maybe waiting and boundaries are less about being told to and more about valuing ourselves enough to.

FOR FURTHER MUSING AND DISCUSSION

1. What is your initial impression when you hear the word *boundaries*?
2. How have guy/girl friendships played out in your life, and most likely based on this, what are your reactions to the thoughts shared about guy/girl friendships in this chapter?
3. What does this sentence mean to you? "Maybe waiting and boundaries are less about being told to and more about valuing ourselves enough to."

Who Am I? by Dietrich Bonhoeffer

Who am I? They often tell me
I stepped from my cell's confinement
Calmly, cheerfully, firmly,
Like a squire from his country-house.
Who am I? They often tell me
I used to speak to my warders
Freely and friendly and clearly,
As though it were mine to command.
Who am I? They also tell me
I bore the days of misfortune
Equally, smilingly, proudly,
Like one accustomed to win.

Am I then really all that which other men tell of?
Or am I only what I myself know of myself?
Restless and longing and sick, like a bird in a cage,
Struggling for breath, as though hands were
compressing my throat,
Yearning for colors, for flowers, for the voices of birds,
Thirsting for words of kindness, for neighborliness,
Tossing in expectation of great events,
Powerlessly trembling for friends at an infinite distance,
Weary and empty at praying, at thinking, at making,
Faint, and ready to say farewell to it all?

Who am I? This or the other?
Am I one person today and tomorrow another?
Am I both at once? A hypocrite before others,
And before myself a contemptibly woebegone weakling?
Or is something within me still like a beaten army,
Fleeing in disorder from victory already achieved?
Who am I? They mock me, these lonely questions of mine.
Whoever I am, Thou knowest, O God, I am Thine!

CHAPTER 14

GUILTY AND FORGIVEN

Draw near to God, and he will draw near to you. Cleanse your hands, you sinners, and purify your hearts, you double-minded.

JAMES 4:8

You bring new life to barren spaces. God who heals, You bring beauty to broken places. Love revealed. I'm not the same since I looked into Your face. You took away all the shame of every time I cursed Your name.

CLARK AND SALINA BEASLEY

SOMETIMES LINES OF the Bible will strike me as odd or flat-out antithetical to what I imagine God was trying to say. Psalm 145:21 recently realized itself as one these: "My mouth will speak the praise of the LORD, and all flesh will bless His holy name forever and ever" (NASB; various other translations say "my flesh"). I'm okay with the first part, but the second part jolts me to question the psalmist's theology and sobriety: "David, I think you mixed up your thoughts here, bud. You're right on with speaking God's praises and blessing His holy name for ever and ever, but then you throw in this flesh part. Flesh can't bless anything but itself. It defines the 'bad, ugly, fallen, sinful, wretched man am I' category. And it hates God and is rightfully opposed to blessing. Right?" Yes according to many pulpits and much popular thought, but no according to the whole of God's Word.

Many of my days begin with *The Divine Hours*,[1] joining myself to fixed prayers prayed throughout the ages. And about the time I started wrestling with David's seeming inebriations, the *Hours* had me repeating this appointed prayer for the week: "O God, who wonderfully created, and yet more wonderfully restored, the dignity of human nature: Grant that we may share the divine life of Him who humbled Himself to share our humanity, your Son Jesus Christ; who lives and reigns with you, in the unity of the Holy Spirit, one God, for ever and ever. Amen."

What's being said here is extraordinary, namely that Jesus' humanity doesn't rupture His divinity but rather recapitulates what God foretold of humanity and divinity from the beginning. An infinite chasm fell between these identities such that none could find, work, or fix his way to the other. We deserved to die (see Genesis 2:17). But by God's grace, a justifying sacrifice and intervention, we may now live. Though Scripture reveals remaining consequence for those in rebellion from God, His nearness is offered as a gift to those who draw near to Him in repentance (see Hebrews 7:25; James 4:8). Immanuel, flesh-and-blood divinity, repaved humanity's way, inviting restoration and reunion with and through the Trinity.

Yes, our human nature falls infinitely short of divine nature. And yes, our sinfulness impairs the lens by which we see every waking moment. But neither of these was a blip on God's radar screen. He created and He creates and, more wonderfully, He restored and is still restoring. Until we believe that every part of us can bless God, including our bodies and sexuality, we're living a half-truth. Until we believe that our creaturely days have as much potential to radiate, receive, and be restored in God's divine love as anything else, we're stuck in a false theology. Love chooses me in my twistedness and channels grace toward where I am and calls me holy, not because I'm no longer twisted or because my twisting came undone but because Love is not overwhelmed by my twisting. I am made to be untwisted by Love.

Many pulpits still preach that only when I shape up will God be able to exist in my presence (usually referenced by Jesus' saying, "My God, my God, why have you forsaken me?" [Psalm 22:1; Matthew 27:46; Mark 15:34]). Sermons settle on an interpretation of God turning from Jesus because the weight of the world's sin (borne by Jesus on the cross) was too much for God to handle. The interpretation I agree more with, however, exposes a moment of Jesus' humanity, where He felt abandoned by His Father. "Based on every iota of pain and fear that surrounds me, there is no way God is here," He seems to say. Jesus felt the suffocating floods of aloneness and forsaking that at some point each of us encounters, screaming the ultimate plea that each of us was, in fact, made for: presence. So either my deepest fear of being inescapably alone has come true or my most outlandish, often unrecognizable hope that God is actually here is, in fact, the truth.

Whether I've done/said/eaten/worked/spent/thought/tried/lied/ excused/served/escaped/heard/hid/handled too much or too little, I can find a way to feel guilty about it. And when I buy into guilt, Jesus will never be enough; the work of His cross seems a pale insufficiency to the depth of my sin. In times that I slip, I can either compromise for a lesser god (see Exodus 20:4; Leviticus 19:4; 1 Chronicles 16:26; Psalm 115:4; 1 Corinthians 10:14), berating the awful sinner who let God (and her guard) down, or I can be gentle on the loved saint (see Psalm 30:4; 34:9; 85:8; Romans 1:7; 8:27; Ephesians 1:1,18; 3:18; Philippians 1:1; Colossians 1:12) who got sidetracked by sin (see Romans 7:19-20). I can receive the condemnation and suffer in my ash, or I can believe the resurrection as alive (see 1 Peter 3:18; Revelation 1:18), turning ashes to beauty (see Isaiah 61:3).

The most unforgiving people I know are those who've yet to forgive themselves. Where you are is not solely your fault, nor is it solely in your capacity to fix. Where you are is reflective of a life of influences, impact, and habituation, and only the One who made you—who has walked behind you, with you, and before you—knows your most suited way from here. Blaming won't heal you and neither will bingeing, hiding, berating, or repressing.

Some form of the cross will mark our every path—some way in which the pain of a broken world intersects our divine call. There are things we wish we'd done differently or decisions we might now call unwise. But living in our regret keeps us from a confident stance in our present and future. Nothing can separate you from the love of God in Christ Jesus (see Romans 8:38-39), and God is for you, not against you (see Romans 8:31). Not an ounce of His being wants less than the best for your life. Can you open to courage and grace enough to receive that, surrendering to these realities written precisely for you?

For me, forgiveness and surrender often involve visualizing in my hands whatever I'm wrestling with (a memory, an action, a feeling, a person) and handing it over. In such handing over, I'm freed up, no longer bound and yet continuing in the lifelong binding of learning to be forgiven, searched (see Psalm 139:23), and surrendered in my prone-to-wander ways. I ask God to lead me and help me surrender my own lead to His. I say aloud, "My body is Yours before it is mine. My sexuality is Yours before it is mine. My mind, heart, actions, day, calendar, and friendships are Yours before they are mine, Father. Help me practice these truths. Lead me in Your everlasting ways. Let Thy will be done in me today, as it is in Thee." And I still don't fully get Him, or me, or us, completely, but what I am getting is more cooperative—more kosher with His Spirit and more unafraid of the raging spirits within me.

The prophet Isaiah said it's too small of a thing for us to just be a servant to God (see Isaiah 49:6). And I imagine this had something to do with servants living in fear—living behind restriction and rules versus living in freedom. We've been called out of darkness (see Psalm 107:14; 2 Corinthians 4:6; 1 Peter 2:9) and into light. Darkness will always fight us, scaring us back into servanthood and keeping us captive to what is not real.

Darkness forces me into hiding and further forces my fear of coming out. Or falling. Or failing. Or death. Or loneliness. Or success. Or not living up. Or letting down. Or indirection. Or too much direction. Or the truth. Or weakness. Or being hurt. Or commitment. Something is always inhibiting me from moving forward, stepping back, or standing still because I'm scared of something else. Something of my greatest fear is always hiding me from my most guttural joy. And something of my greatest freedom always waits in my most coveted trepidation. Hope, then, fails in seeking God in this midst.

Consider what Jesus did for one afflicted man He met:

> After these things there was a feast of the Jews, and Jesus went up to Jerusalem. Now there is in Jerusalem by the sheep gate a pool, which is called in Hebrew Bethesda, having five porticoes. In these lay a multitude of those who were sick, blind, lame, and withered, waiting for the moving of the waters; for an angel of the Lord went down at certain seasons into the pool and stirred up the water; whoever then first, after the stirring up of the water, stepped in was made well from whatever disease with which he was afflicted. A man was there who had been ill for thirty-eight years. When Jesus saw him lying there, and knew that he had already been a long time in that condition, He said to him, "Do you wish to get well?" The sick man answered Him, "Sir, I have no man to put me into the pool when the water is stirred up, but while I am coming, another steps down before me." Jesus said to him, "Get up, pick up your pallet and walk." Immediately the man became well, and picked up his pallet and began to walk. (John 5:1-9, NASB)

In some ways, I get that God wants me to be well and that He's powerful enough to provide that wellness. What I don't get is His compassion, well aware of what I did last night or the last 1,700 nights, and His continued desire to be with me. God pursues me even in my disobedience. I don't have to regain His attention by fancying myself up with lacy lingerie or smooth talking. But what I do have to do is offer myself to His attention—to Immanuel's courtship, waiting for and wanting to be with me.

Our temptation in handling guilt runs the gamut of blame, fixing, performing, and serving our way back to stable ground. Don't get me wrong: Tenacity is great, *until* fatigue, effort, and shame start paving your road to Calvary. Doing is easier than not doing, though, and legalism is easier than freedom. Doing judges me in light of what I've done; freedom asks me to believe that on the basis of Christ's doing, I am forgiven. I've been reading the journals of Mother Teresa lately, and, wow, that woman had fight. She's teaching me much about links between tenacity, the kingdom of God, and salvation by faith (see 1 Peter 1:9; Acts 26:18; Romans 3:28–5:2; Galatians 2:16,20; Hebrews 11:4), not obedience—being saved by grace, not good works (see Romans 9:31-32; Ephesians 2:9). Before I am called God's servant, I am called His daughter. And before I am called to serve broken souls, I am called to the humble task of tending to my own soul. Only one person was meant to be crucified, not two.

What about my rebellion and the conscious choice to choose love and lovers other than God? "Like the woman I speak of in Hosea 3," I almost hear Him say, "who was loved by her husband yet was an adulteress, turning to other gods? Or like the Israelites, or Peter, who walked with Me in person for a number of years and still denied the realities of My love?"

What about all the fallen hours of my past or addictions to licentiousness and pleasure? What about my injustice, intolerance, pride, selfishness, greed, gluttony, perjury, covetous lust, perfectionism, envy, adultery, abuse, malice, gossip, addiction, wrongful attraction, speeding, running a red light, cheating, telling white lies, exaggerating, boasting, breaking any law, buying too much, giving with ill motives, false motivation, faking, forging? What about my identity as a "sinner"?

"I no longer identify you as a sinner, Abbie. You're a saint who sins.[2] Nothing can trump My cross. No past, present addiction, lust, licentiousness, or gluttonized pleasure is beyond my handling or alters my pursuit of you and desire to welcome you Home" (see Luke 15:11-32).

A. W. Tozer said, "What comes into our minds when we think about God is the most important thing about us."[3] An interesting twist on this is considering what comes into God's mind when He thinks about you or, more bizarrely, when He prays for you (see John 17; Romans 8:26-27). What would it look like to envision God holding your body, speaking forgiveness and freedom into each part that you abhor? What if I internalized that I am not a burden to God and that He can handle me, just as I am?

The most heinous act in history happened between a tender hand and a piece of fruit, and I would've picked it too. But the Truth says I am forgiven (see Matthew 9:2; Luke 5:20; 7:48) and still allowed abundant life (see John 7:38; Romans 5:17; Revelation 7:17). I can't get pretty, smart, strong, or solid enough to change Truth's plan, let alone mess up enough hours of my life to cause it to be forsaken (see Ephesians 2:8). If God is the God He says He is, He is with me for the duration (see Genesis 26:3; 31:3; Exodus 3:12; Joshua 1:5; Judges 6:16; 1 Kings 11:38; Isaiah 43:2), in my strength and in my weakness (see Luke 22:61), in my compliance and in my wandering (see Luke 15:17-21). The question is, do I really trust God's words as true?

FOR FURTHER MUSING AND DISCUSSION

1. Which do you tend to feel more often, guilty or forgiven?
2. What refreshing aspects of God did this chapter communicate to you?
3. In what areas do you still feel confused, impure, condemned, or unsure?
4. Spend some time reading Psalm 139.

Where I have so punished, let me so Love.

Where I have lived in fear, teach me Freedom.

Where I have restricted, help me trust the Table before me.

Where I have hurt others, teach me to Confess.

Where I have hurt myself, teach me Healing, unloosing the
hands from around my neck.

Where I have been hurt, teach me to Forgive.

Where I have controlled, show me Surrender.

Where I am alone, let me be Embraced.

Where I remain tired, lead me to the gift of Rest.

Where I remain afraid of tomorrow or ashamed by yesterday,
unveil to me the gift of Grace today.

WITH LOVE, YOUR DAUGHTER

CHAPTER 15

MASTURBATION AND CHASTITY

The aim of our charge is love that issues from a pure heart and a good conscience and a sincere faith.

1 TIMOTHY 1:5

Sexual expression means much more than mere "sex," than doing or not doing "it." The single male and the single female, who live with the Lord as their center, witness to the wholeness of the masculine and of the feminine and to the way in which these two sides of being human complement each other.

WENDY SHALIT

When you are interiorly free, you call others to freedom, whether you know it or not. Freedom attracts wherever it appears. A free man or a free woman creates a space where others feel safe and want to dwell. Our world is so full of conditions, demands, requirements, and obligations that we often wonder what is expected of us. But when we meet a truly free person, there are no expectations, only an invitation to reach into ourselves and discover there our own freedom. Where true inner freedom is, there is God. And where God is, there we want to be.

HENRI NOUWEN

SOME OF YOU flipped here first, wanting answers to your masturbation dilemmas. I probably would've done the same thing. Before diving in to those conversations, though, please consider and keep these words at a forefront as you probe these pages: Rules are easier than freedom, and hatred is easier than love. Love will always be a mystery, and most of my fear will always reside in the parts of me that seem mysterious. Rules, answers, and models are helpful approximations, but they're earthly renditions and fall short. They can be helpful pointers, but when taken on as our rule, they act as dangerous competitors with true perfection. The best of our makeshift reflections crumble in comparison with face-to-face union (see 1 Corinthians 13:12), holiness, humility, submission, oneness, uniqueness, equality, and equally unique individuality. And these are the basis for this chapter. Our hearts are perverted in all their attempts. No matter how disciplined or devout we are, our motivations are skewed—trapped in deceptions of our flesh that is tainted by shrapnel of the Fall. We are inclined toward religion and restriction—naturally bent toward tendencies to condemn and punish ourselves. God knows this—knew this—from the beginning and paved our rescue. "Now, with God's help," said Søren Kierkegaard, "I shall become myself."

In Christ, and only in Christ, do we find freedom to become ourselves, not because of ourselves but because of Christ and Christ's love in the Father (see John 17; Colossians 2). In Christ, and only in Christ, do we find an identity by which we're able to receive and freely impart to others, not for the sake of our own gain but for gain of Another. In Christ, we find a worth in ourselves lineaged to a worth beyond ourselves; we find a radically hopeful and eternal invitation to being and becoming our true selves, here and now. How does this relate to masturbation? Well, some of that I will try to unpack, but some of it I simply cannot put into words.

It is easier to get honest conversation from nonreligious people regarding topics such as masturbation. Among other things, there's nothing at stake for them and they really have no reason *not* to be honest. Some Christians, on the other hand, nearly turn into clams when asked about it. Centuries past have equated sexual promiscuity and masturbation with mental instability, among other things. The fifteenth century saw an influx of people inflicted with syphilis, which, left untreated, was said to bring insanity and even sexual promiscuity, including masturbation (particularly for individuals who either worked at or frequented brothels). As a result, cages were fitted over sleeping boys' genitals, and young girls prone to sexual stimulation were given clitoridectomies (removal of the clitoris). Scholars practicing in the fields of medicine and science have long considered masturbation intrinsic and natural to our bodily makeup, while many leaders in the church have tended to call it an inconceivable wrong.

Advocates against masturbation often base their stance on Genesis 38, a story about Onan (whose name roots the ancient etymology of masturbation, *onanism*). Following the custom of the day, Onan submitted to marrying his deceased brother's wife (then a widow). He refuted the custom, however, at the point of bearing her children to the continued line of his dead brother: "Onan knew that the offspring would not be his; so whenever he lay with his brother's wife, he spilled his semen on the ground to keep from producing offspring for his brother. What he did was wicked in the LORD's sight; so he put him to death" (verses 9-10, NIV). Onan wasn't punished for *masturbation* but rather, it should be noted, failure to uphold Hebraic Law (see Deuteronomy 25:5-10). Masturbation has never been understood, let alone preached, with consistent conclusions or reason. Consider the following opinions on masturbation:

-   Richard Dobbins, who wrote *Teaching Your Children the Truth About Sex*, takes an approach that neither condemns nor condones the act, determining its ethics multifactorally.[1] Dr. James Dobson said,

> It is my opinion that masturbation is not much of an issue with God. It's a normal part of adolescence, which involves no one else. It does not cause disease, it does not produce babies, and Jesus did not mention it in the Bible. I'm not telling you to masturbate, and I hope you won't feel the need for it. The best thing I can do is suggest that you talk to God personally about this matter and decide what He wants you to do.[2]

From a Christ-following college professor:

In a case where one becomes obsessive about masturbation — like any kind of obsession — one ought to get therapy. Some have suggested that masturbation is simply selfish sex and therefore wrong. I do not think the issue is as simple as all that. It may be that my bodily desire allows me to hardly think about anything else but sex. If I am really hungry, or thirsty, or tired, I can hardly think about anything else but food or drink or sleep. There is nothing self-serving about taking the edge off these desires so I can concentrate on serving others with limited distraction. So, too, with sexual desire and the single person. No sincere Christian will go out and look for another person to use for sexual gratification. Think of all these stories in the news over the last few years where teachers unable to control their desires have been predatory towards their students and have burdened those students with very difficult psychological trauma. Nevertheless, to relieve oneself takes the edge off the desire and doesn't take advantage of others. Someone might object, "But sex is reserved for two people in marriage, so doesn't masturbation teach one to find pleasure without another?" Perhaps. But it might also make it possible to keep oneself out of an illicit sexual union in order to preserve one for a sexual relationship with one's life partner. It also allows one to explore and understand better how his or her body works so when marriage does come one is better prepared.

From a pastor:

I once advocated against masturbation. It had been a part of my life prior to my becoming a Christian. After I came to Christ, I felt guilty about it because I couldn't engage in the practice without imagining being in union with someone. I felt these imaginative visuals must be wrong. I confided in my struggle with a pastor friend, and he told me simply not to do it. So, wanting to walk with Jesus, I didn't. I stopped completely for five years. Until I got married, I did not masturbate or do anything to assert myself sexually, even though the desire to do so was very, very strong.

What occurred during those five years did give me some pause and left me wondering about many things. First of all, a man's body has cycles like a woman's. It is about a seven-day cycle rather than the 28-day cycle you women have. The intensity of male desire peaks after about three days and remains so high-pitched that a guy feels like he wants to crawl out of his skin. This lasts for about seven days. If a man does not have sex (if married) or relieve himself, he can hardly concentrate on much else. It is simply the way God wired us. Furthermore, if a man does not have some kind of release, his body does it automatically in his sleep. This is what is meant by a "wet dream." In his sleep, so it is completely involuntary, a man will dream that he is making love to someone and will have an orgasm. The dream comes with visuals. It is neither sought nor manufactured. It is simply the way a man's body works.

I am convinced that Jesus' body did this too and think it is Gnostic and Docetic to suggest otherwise. I am sure He had orgasms because He had a genuine human body with all of the bodily functions any other man would have. The Scriptures are explicit also that He never once colored outside the lines and did something He wasn't supposed to do. But, anyway, years after I was married, I started trying to put the pieces together more honestly and came to the belief that masturbation was probably not wrong. The difficulty for such a view, however, is the fact that when a man masturbates, he generates his own visuals as he does so. So now the question is, are the imagined visuals wrong? They may be, pure and simple, but I'm not so sure it is all that simple. In the Scriptures, there are references to men enjoying the breasts of the wife of their youth. How do you read that and not imagine a breast? There are texts that talk about circumcision; how does a woman read that and not imagine a penis? There are texts in the Song of Solomon that are descriptions of lovemaking and it is unequivocal; how does one read that and not think about two people copulating?

I think visuals can become pornographic, but they are not necessarily so. The pornographic is an abuse of images. It is another topic altogether and one I have thought much about, but maybe it is for another time. Suffice it to say, pornography is designed to play on human weakness and the pornographer is also trying to capitalize on that weakness. It is utilitarian and uses others. In fact, it is this kind of violation of the boundaries of others that features so significantly in virtually all sexual abuse in any form. Lust is often confused with sexual desire. Sexual desire isn't lust any more than hunger is gluttony. Lust, in its biblical sense, is predatory; it seeks to entrap and use another person for one's own pleasure. This is when it becomes wrong. The church, then, does well when it can affirm folks in the fact that they are sexual beings instead of engaging in teachings that either deny or suppress the reality. Furthermore, the church can help by teaching and guiding singles to develop spiritual disciplines so they will learn how to manage the intensity of their desires and grow spiritually strong in the process. Furthermore, the church can help singles harness all of that sexual energy and direct it toward reaching out to neighbors, getting on board with a social justice issue, or perhaps working with victims of sexual predators to help them reign in their own desires so as not to express them inappropriately.

A rebuttal to this from one of my editors:

I'm not sure any of that has to do with masturbation. In other words, it attempts to answer a question, which most assume to be something of a gray area, by moving into areas that are much more gray. If sexual activity was created as a means of union and communion — not self-gratification — then masturbation is, by necessity, a warped and twisted response to sexual desire. It is self-affirming rather than union-affirming, which is the very sin (at least in my mind). Therefore, it is irrelevant to talk about whether or not one is thinking of sexual images; that has nothing to do with deciding if it is a sin. It is a sin because it demeans the design; it trains the body to find satisfaction in a union-creating act without the union. At its heart, masturbation, just like pornography (though in different ways), dehumanizes the act of sex.

Why do we feel guilty about this thing so much more so than a lot of other things in Christian circles? Is there something that is a good, honest spiritual conviction in it? Is that where the guilt comes from? Or is it simply our culture that creates that "yeah, this is probably wrong" mentality in us? I think it's one of those things for which we'll meet Jesus face-to-face and realize how silly and small and dumb it was to get hung up on. I think for some people, it can really turn that corner into obsession and gluttony and an improper fulfillment of God-given needs. But at the end of it, I think we have bigger spiritual fish to fry.

Regardless of one's conclusions, understandings of masturbation are unequivocally linked to understandings of one's self, Christ, and one's self in Christ. Similarly, understandings of chastity cannot be situated apart from understandings of who Jesus is and how He relates to the Father and Spirit or how our identity plays and interplays into that of the Father, Son, and Holy Spirit. As Lauren Winner wrote,

> Usual strategies for helping people cope with sexuality are not working, repeating biblical teachings about sex is simply not enough, urging self-discipline is not enough, reminding people of the psychological cost of premarital sex or infidelity is not enough. What we need is something larger and deeper: a clear vision of what chastity ultimately is and the most important context in which it is to be practiced. . . . Chastity is doing sex in the body of Christ — doing sex in a way that befits the body of Christ — and that keeps you grounded, and bounded, in the community. Chastity is a basic rule of the community, but it is not a mere rule. It is also discipline. Chastity is something you do; it is something you practice. It is not only a state — the state of being chaste — but a disciplined, active undertaking that we do as part of the body.[3]

Joining in the discipline of chastity and taking to the proposals of the triune God literally means shifting one's primary family and personal identity to that which is eternal — that which is God's — and integrally part of God's Body, the church. Earthly ties become secondary to eternal ties, in Christ, and we're able to partake of (among other virtuous fruits) self-control, contentedness, fulfillment, and union. Our lives have been given invitation to live with and within the larger life and relationship of Christ. And as Christians, our highest call comes in fulfillment of this with and within—of this abiding in true love, union with our truest Lover. According to Winner,

> Understanding chastity as a discipline helps us quiet that nagging voice in our heads that says, "I'm being made to give up something that is totally normal and natural!" Of course, the desire for sex is normal and natural, but many spiritual disciplines—the so-called disciplines of abstinence—center on refraining from something normal. . . . The unmarried Christian who practices chastity refrains from sex in order to remember that God desires your person, your body, more than any man or woman ever will.[4]

Lust misuses sex for personal gratification, uprooting it from God's intended purposes. Chastity, then, should rightly involve a proper use of sex and stewarding of one's sexuality, rooted in giving and grounded in God's intended purposes. That said, my journey toward becoming chaste has been inseparable from my journey of becoming sexual, and my journey in becoming sexual has been inseparable from my journey toward becoming chaste. And both have been inseparable from my journey of becoming human.

Understanding my sexuality has allowed me to be satisfied in my chastity, and understanding my chastity has allowed me to freely explore my sexuality. My sexual personhood is vital to my being human, a human imaged by God. Differentiating my sexuality as a female, my sensuality as a woman, and my righteousness as God's daughter has brought me face-to-face with my image and His—face-to-face with desires to be chaste and abilities to channel chastity toward my neighbor and living out Christ's story.

For me, chastity is being able to feel sexual and feel my sexuality based in my humanity and expressed apart from sexual intercourse, or, as the *Renovaré Spiritual Formation Bible* defines it, "purposefully turning away for a time from dwelling upon or engaging in the sexual dimension of our relationship to others—even our husband or wife—and thus learning how not to be governed by this powerful aspect of our life."[5] This could embody an alternative physical release, such as jogging or dancing, or engaging in something communal, such as serving a neighbor or dining with friends. It could mean acknowledging the joys of a sensual bath, good food, or a massage. Or maybe it means opening myself to pleasures found in beauty, texture, or creation. Or maybe it looks like downloading a sermon, listening to worshipful music, or reading passionate Scripture. All such means (known to psychologists as "sublimation") promote fleeing from sexual immorality (see 1 Corinthians 6:18) and renewing one's mind (see Romans 12:2) in Christ. C. S. Lewis said,

> We may, indeed, be sure that perfect chastity — like perfect charity — will not be attained by any merely human efforts. You must ask for God's help. Even when you have done so, it may seem to you for a long time that no help, or less help than you need, is being given. Never mind. After each failure, ask forgiveness, pick yourself up, and try again. Very often what God first helps us towards is not the virtue itself but just this power of always trying again. For however important chastity (or courage, or truthfulness, or any other virtue) may be, this process trains us in habits of the soul, which are more important still. It cures our illusions about ourselves and teaches us to depend on God. We learn, on the one hand, that we cannot trust ourselves even in our best moments, and, on the other hand, that we need not despair even in our worst, for our failures are forgiven.[6]

Like any other practice, masturbation is a form of training. It trains us toward something and away from something else. So our question must be, is the particular training I'm giving myself to moving me toward God and a kingdom mindset or away from Him? Far from being a question of what the body is doing and what the heart is doing, masturbation is a question of what I am giving myself to and how I am offering my life as a living sacrifice (see Romans 12:1). Furthermore, am I walking in light of the powers given to me herein — the actual life of God and energy that grounds and orients relations between the

Father, Son, and Spirit, living in me (see Acts 17:28; Galatians 2:20; 5:16-25)?

At a Christian conference, a brave young soul had the courage to ask two prominent women in today's Christian circles what their thoughts were for those who struggle with masturbation. Both speakers got flustered, eyeing each other with the look of, "Did she really just ask that in public? And how are we supposed to respond?"

After some awkwardness, one of the women said, "Um, honestly, I don't know if I can say the *m* word. It just feels so . . . beyond me. Granted, I'm a married woman, but I've just never understood why people do that." At this point, she turned to the other speaker and asked if she had anything to add.

"No . . . definitely not. Just keep yourselves pure from it, and God will protect you."

In a matter of few words and body language, a courageous girl and audience were shut down in their sexuality. Honest vulnerability was met with everything but compassion and validation of sexuality's complexity. When sexual temptation, including masturbation, comes this audience's way, the words "it is bad" will likely be recalled. And, more specifically, paralyzing translations of "I am bad" will leave them in shame rather than leading them toward Truth.

When I imagine this girl asking Jesus the same question, even in a crowd of antagonists, or coming from the mouth of a prostitute, I imagine Him looking deep in her eyes and searching her longing soul, maybe kneeling down and putting His hands on her face, disarming evident fears. I imagine Him using tender, empowering words such as, "Go and sin no more," while scribing grace and forgiveness into the sand beneath her (see John 8:1-11). When we're unable to enter the mind of one who masturbates—let alone one who is a sex addict, prostitute, cutter, killer, rapist, has had an abortion—there's a detachment between who Jesus was and who we're presuming to follow.

God desires to be with us, as we are, letting Him adore us in that place. He isn't opposed to, or afraid of, talking about subjects we call "touchy," such as sex or masturbation, evidenced by His stepping out of heaven to engage with this realm we call "life" and "living as a human." He didn't always heal the immediate issue before Him, but He was always *with*—always awakened to the present and to the presence of true Love in that moment. Maybe Jesus knew that something about *being truly with* was the unbelievably healing presence that we long for.

FOR FURTHER MUSING AND DISCUSSION

1. What stands out to you in this quote from Henri Nouwen?

> When you are interiorly free, you call others to freedom, whether you know it or not. Freedom attracts wherever it appears. A free man or a free woman creates a space where others feel safe and want to dwell. Our world is so full of conditions, demands, requirements, and obligations that we often wonder what is expected of us. But when we meet a truly free person, there are no expectations, only an invitation to reach into ourselves and discover there our own freedom. Where true inner freedom is, there is God. And where God is, there we want to be.

What do you think this has to do with sexuality?

2. When considering the views on masturbation, which one(s) stood out to you?

3. What comes to mind when you hear the word *chastity*? How does the following definition support or challenge what you just shared?

> chastity: "Purposefully turning away for a time from dwelling upon or engaging in the sexual dimension of our relationship to others — even our husband or wife — and thus learning how not to be governed by this powerful aspect of our life." (*The Renovaré Spiritual Formation Bible*)

4. A healthy sexuality is about being able to feel a desire or recognize a longing—definitely a sexual one—and explore it with God. In praying about the longing, you could simply ask, "What might you be inviting me to here, Lord, or showing me about my longing or dissatisfaction? Furthermore, am I okay even admitting that I have longings and desires that are out of my control?" What arises in you at the thought of putting these prayers into practice this week?

5. What's challenging to you about imagining that God can handle our conversations about sexuality? What's freeing to you about that same image?

Sometimes it is necessary to reteach a thing its loveliness, to put a hand on its brow of the flower and retell it in words and in touch it is lovely until it flowers again from within.

GALWAY KINNELL

CHAPTER 16

WAITING WELL

I wait for the LORD, my soul waits, and in his word I hope; my soul waits for the Lord more than watchmen for the morning, more than watchmen for the morning. O Israel, hope in the LORD! For with the LORD there is steadfast love, and with him is plentiful redemption.

PSALM 130:5-7

The place God calls you to is the place where your deep gladness and the world's deep hunger meet.

FREDERICK BUECHNER

FOR A WHILE, I thought God had forgotten His will for my life, so I tried to help remind Him. On the husband front, I'd give Him some ideas and remind Him of the type I'm attracted to. I'd make lists of what was negotiable and what wasn't—characteristics I wouldn't compromise on and those that were up for grabs. Then I'd tell God, "My will is ready, so whenever You want to come along and bless it, that'd be swell." The following was written on one of these occasions:

It was a slow Saturday morning, where sleeping in and daydreaming to the pillow was at its best. Thoughts of "the husband" couldn't help but amuse me, less in a lonely appeal (at least this day) and more in a "Wow, someday times like this will be sweet to share with my best friend. I wonder what it'll be like. I wonder what he'll be like. Will he serenade me out of bed, or will he let us lie for a while and then request a hearty breakfast and hiking at a nearby mountain?" I mention these two (singing and athleticism) because they've highlighted a large part of my "list" lately. Selfishly, I want my husband to be athletic, and it'd be really fun if he were a musician, too. I eventually let my spiritual side catch up to my daydreams, and God wanted to pry a little deeper.

"Out of curiosity, would I [God] make your cut? Would I survive your set of standards? Clearly, I'd score well on your nonnegotiables. In fact, I think I'd quite characterize their fullness (godliness, purity, integrity, faith, desire, love, commitment, and respect for you), but My greater concern is making the cut for any of your "negotiables," which seems to say that from the start, you're going to be let down — even with God as your hypothetical husband? I mean, I had My day as a decent fisherman, but as for being supremely athletic, the jury's still out. And this worship-leader bit — I understand that it's appealing, but realize that their doing so is an extraction of their actual selves — a fringe element (musical gifting) of their real garment. Again, I can strike a darn good tune in the shower, but stick me in front of a crowd and the fat lady sung, a long time ago. Let me put it this way, and then you can get back to daydreaming: Think about how many of My athletic or musical talents were recorded. None. Nada. Zippo. Apparently, nothing about My profile status — looks, talents, salary, hobbies — was worth writing down. What's favorable to the world isn't necessarily so to Me. Call Me arrogant, but I'm the only one who really knows what you need, let alone will provide it."

When the love I long for fits between the lines of an 8.5-by-11-inch sheet of paper, I've realized that my understandings are depleted and distorted and need to be renegotiated.

If I were God, I'd live for at least five thousand years, heal every creature, and make sure every creature was secure, healthy, equal, and equally treated. I'd be the best thinker, athlete, architect, model, scientist, cook, singer, communicator, doctor, actress, nurturer, artist, dentist, mathematician, historian—well, I'll stop with that because

I'd clearly be the most humble, too. And when I thought my reign was nearing its end, I'd throw a worldwide going-out party and die peacefully in the quiet confines of my (mountainously dropped on the north, sandy beaches on the south, urban on the east, and countryside on the west) home.

Apparently, Jesus and I think differently.

Jesus could have been superb at anything, but for whatever reason, He chose the more unnatural road, a sacrificial one of emptying toward nothing (see Philippians 2:6-8). The Trinity's flesh lived a less-than-average lifespan and died an abhorrent death, stepping out of perfection only to reign as a servant, be crucified as a criminal, and resurrect in virtual secrecy. From what we're told, Jesus chose not to be known as a famous fisherman, debater, carpenter, or even preacher. Rather, He chose to be known as simply Himself. Apparently being ourselves is priceless.[1]

For all of us — married and divorced, dated much and dated none at all, engaged, widowed, or just broken up — our ongoing task remains to seek, ask for, and proactively wait on God's pursuit, learning to believe that His courtship is where our greatest hope, rest, and desire fall. A paraphrase of Saint Augustine says that God made us for Himself, and until our rest is found in Him, we'll be restless. In other words, on this side of heaven my deepest thirst is for a union that will never be quenched. Certain intimacies will impressively compete, but something in me will remain dehydrated, cut off from true vitality.[2] In states of bad, good, and mediocre waiting, however, there will always be a Lover at hand — a promise that Love is leading a better way (see Romans 8:28).

I used to get exhausted by the mysteries of love. "It's such a risk, God. I can't do it anymore." But I'm slowly understanding that love is not the risk; life is what's the risk. Life is unpredictable and unprecedented. It's a deception (see Isaiah 41:29; Jeremiah 9:6; 10:14), making neither promises that will come to fruition nor aspirations that will last more than a breath. Life apart from God seduces death and, in the end, dies herself. Life will fail us, hurt us, abuse us, and hold us wrongly. She will tell us things that are not true and treat us in ways that are not fair. Life will be evil and always a risk. Yet when I'm able to secure my risks in life to the realities of God and hope in His unseen territories, love and faith and true Life awaken — life with God (see Hebrews 11:1).

Founded upon God's self-revelation — namely the Cross — we find that many acts of love are equally acts of condemnation. The Cross proclaims sin as much as it proclaims love, not in a frightening, minimizing, or schizophrenic way but rather in a way that sharpens what True Love really is and tells and does. When I am willing to grapple with my atoned-for sainthood, while remaining addicted to this world, Love is victorious and death is no more (see Revelation 21:4).

God's love tells me that in life I will lose. I will always end up short or hurting, not because I failed at life but because I was created having lost the battle. But I was also created to be fought for and won over by a Savior. Love is difficult because love changes the course of our lives, drawing us out and leaving us vulnerable. We'd rather hide behind big, flashy, pretty, relevant, hip, rich, growing lifestyles than seek contentment in who we are and who God designed us to be. And it's possible to skate through life in these postures, not letting Love change the navigation of your life — not letting God romance you back to Him.

But when we meet True Love, our most fantastic defenses fall. Pursuing a knowledge of Him and a knowledge of ourselves alongside communion with God and communion with His saints will change us, causing us to realize that God is worth waiting for and we have worth enough to wait. Don't give up on God, and don't believe the lie that God has given up on you. Whether in relation to your singleness or something entirely different, Love never fails. As we stand at the door (see Revelation 3:20), knocking for daily bread (see Matthew 6:11) or kneeling for today's sustenance, it is He (see John 10:9) who hears and answers (see Matthew 7:7). It is He who's the substitution providing us the power to wait, and wait well, for our eternal Home and actual Marriage.[3] He, in fact, is the One we're waiting for: "our blessed hope, the appearing of the glory of our great God and Savior Jesus Christ" (Titus 2:13).

If I'm honest with myself, I want to get married. I want to have sex. I want to grow old with someone. I want to be noticed by someone. I want kids. And my singleness continues to fight with God on these fronts for clarity and right perspective: "You're the One who designed me with these instincts, God, and the One causing an empty womb and unsigned wedding certificate." But I've guarded these hopes from myself for so long because, well, what if they don't happen? What if this God-figure, whom I've believed for all these years, doesn't pan out and give me the desires of my heart?

Negating our instincts and desires seems a repression of our souls and sadly opposite to God's. Jesus tells us to ask for things and goes on to say that He'll even open doors to such things (see Matthew 7:7-8; Luke 11:9-10). That's what kids do: They *ask* their parents for what they want. And a lot of times their parents give it to them (see Matthew 7:11; Luke 11:13)! But from time to time, a parent knows that perceived needs aren't always actual needs and, in fact, could even be destructive. When petitions become expectations, or answers become obligations, we end up feeling let down and disappointed.

In the end, all longings end in God. Admitting a longing simply says to Him, "Here is a space where I am not satisfied; here is an area of my dreams where I'm struggling to truthfully engage." By doing so, by taking the risk of opening up and voicing grief and longing, space opens up wherein He can move and I can more willingly receive His movements. Life and God's will happen, with or without me. I can't ruin God's plan by asking or acting outside of it, but I can sleep through it, forgetting that staying awake to God means staying awake to an abundance beyond my wildest creativity.

Take my desire to be a mother. When I was about twelve, I got into doing charcoal drawings—more specifically, charcoal drawings of pregnant women. Clearly, I thought (as my parents thought about calling a shrink), women were made to mother. They were maternally sculpted to connect with offspring in a significant way. The women I watch at the park and friends with their children look tired. "But at least they're getting to be tired *as a mom*, God. At least they're getting to do what they're destined for. If only I could exhaust my life toward such an end."

More recently, I've felt freedom from God to *keep drawing*, to keep dreaming about the desires He's put in my heart, to let Him widen concepts of mothering and things maternal. Whether babysitting or watching a couple's kids for the weekend or tossing a Frisbee with the crack-parented seven-year-old from down the street, I've realized, *I'm mothering*. When mentoring someone or inviting a neighbor into my home, I'm mothering. When volunteering at the local children's hospital, coaching a team, or praying for those younger than me, I'm mothering. When considering or maybe one day partaking in fostering or adoption, I'm practicing motherhood—perusing maternal corners of God's heart and certainly mine. In the words of Edith Schaeffer, "If you have no children of your own, you can adopt some for scattered hours in your life, helping them and yourself at the same time."[4] Mothering, I've realized, is an intention or intentional focusing of my heart as much as it is holding a biological baby in my arms. I am a mother by way of my womanhood and God-given identity, not simply by being married with child.

Paul exposed such opportunity toward a single's theology of parenting, proposing a simile about his care for the flock in Thessalonica:

> We proved to be gentle among you, as a nursing mother tenderly cares for her own children. Having so fond an affection for you, we were well-pleased to impart to you not only the gospel of God but also our own lives, because you had become very dear to us. For you recall, brethren, our labor and hardship, how working night and day so as not to be a burden to any of you, we proclaimed to you the gospel of God. You are witnesses, and so is God, how

devoutly and uprightly and blamelessly we behaved toward you believers;
just as you know how we were exhorting and encouraging and imploring
each one of you as a father would his own children, so that you would walk in
a manner worthy of the God who calls you into His own kingdom and glory.

(1 Thessalonians 2:7-12, NASB)

We are God's instruments to remind children of God, whether we're
biological parents or otherwise.

Too many singles spend hours waiting for their futures to unfold
or waiting to let God unfold their futures until the present aligns
with the future they envisioned. But among many problems with
this, waiting doesn't end if a spouse enters the picture. I just got off
the phone with a friend who's been waiting two years for their
adopted baby. Another friend has been waiting two weeks for her
grandfather to leave the ICU. Another to get a job. Another to
become pregnant. And there are many more scenarios. Just ask someone who's married.

Maybe you want to be a doctor but you don't want to commit to
years of schooling or the chance of moving, sans spouse. Or maybe
you dream of having a home, with a kitchen table and flowerpots and
a space for guests to sit for coffee. Maybe you dream of hosting a
dinner party, having a dog, taking a vacation, or having a role in the
church but muzzle it because you're not married. Such muzzling is
unnecessary and, in fact, is in cooperation with a lie told by the
Enemy. In Christ, you are made to image the Creator of the universe.
You are made to taste and see glimpses of your heavenly home, culti-
vating and experiencing cultivations of Him and His notice of you
today.[5] We mustn't forsake our dreams of life and home and living
due to an order of life that's not shaping up as we expected. And we
must be honest with God, sharing with Him tensions of desire and
lament, anger and sadness, grief and hope. We must be willing to
bring laughter and loneliness into the arms of our Father, for this is
where healing begins.

FOR FURTHER MUSING AND DISCUSSION

1. What was challenging to you about this chapter?
2. What was encouraging?
3. What seasons of waiting has God given you? How has He shaped you through these seasons?

What If?

"What if?" said the artist to the viewer.
What if there were a canvas that was finished,
And what if the artist of that canvas showed it to a viewer?

"Wow," the viewer might say, "that's stunning."

"Thank you. That really means a lot," the artist might humbly
respond.

Turning to the piece, however, he shares a chuckling,
questioning, coveting of sorts. "How can he call you stunning,
having viewed you only so briefly? And with such brief
understanding, relative to what we've shared?"

"What if, though," the canvas replied, "he could actually see
something stunning, despite limited perspective of our whole?
What if stunning could be found in a color, curve, or even
corner of us versus seeing the whole of our final masterpiece?
What if part was enough to stun today?
What if stunning was enough to fully realize part?
What if there were a canvas that was finished
And the artist could see the stunning whole but the viewer
could only see part?
And yet what if that part could be called stunning and in many
ways whole?"

"What if?" said the artist to the viewer.

CHAPTER 17

LOVE'S RULE

A man found an eagle's egg and put it in a nest of a barnyard hen. The eaglet hatched with the brood of chicks and grew up with them. All his life the eagle did what the barnyard chicks did, thinking he was a barnyard chicken. He scratched the earth for worms and insects. He clucked and cackled. And he would thrash his wings and fly a few feet into the air.

Years passed and the eagle grew very old. One day he saw a magnificent bird above him in the cloudless sky. It glided in graceful majesty among the powerful wind currents, with scarcely a beat on his strong golden wings. The old eagle looked up in awe. "Who's that?" he asked. "That's the eagle, the king of the birds," said his neighbour. "He belongs to the sky. We belong to the earth — we're chickens." So the eagle lived and died a chicken, for that's what he thought he was.

ANTHONY DE MELLO

Man's whole life is a continual contradiction of what he knows to be his duty.

LEO TOLSTOY

SOMETIMES I WISH God would've put a book in the Bible called "Dating" (as well as "Politics" and "Solving Poverty"). But then I think maybe He didn't for a reason. Maybe He knew there was something more vital than finding a proper spouse, electing the most profitable president, and sourcing clean water. Or maybe He knew that if I had a rubric to tell me how to do something, I'd lose sight of needing Him for anything worth doing. In other words, I often wonder if having an exact (or even vague) idea of what I'm doing with my life isn't quite the cultural gem it's cracked up to be. Maybe there's something treasurable about attempting to follow God rather than merely figuring Him out.

Willingness to lose, or loosen one's reins from, one's faith seems a scriptural means to finding real faith (see John 12:24). My first book was called *Can You Keep Your Faith in College?* I wanted my second to be *Can You Be Willing to Lose Your Faith, Please?* But then I decided people might get the wrong idea. The idea was to say that just maintaining one's faith is not a virtuous goal. To keep something can too easily translate into conforming to a standard we're comfortable with. But Jesus never prescribed such a lukewarm model (see Revelation 3:16). He said something more like, "Faith, hope, and love should be our greatest rule" (1 Corinthians 13:13), and, "Follow Me" (Matthew 4:19; 8:22; 9:9; 16:24; 19:21; Mark 1:17; 2:14; 8:34; 10:21; Luke 5:27; 9:23; 9:59; 18:22; John 1:43; 10:27; 12:26; 21:19).

The challenge is that it's easier to follow rules than to face freedom. So when I'm striving for perfection, I'm trying to control, fix, or resist something—like freedom and grace. If my basis for right standing with God involves following a rule, I will eventually fall short. But if my basis centers around the undefinable shape of a *Person* named Love, the pressure is off. I no longer have to look perfect, have all the answers, or be in control, because *He is.* Mere religion forms moral people who hope they're loved; Christ forms human beings who know they're loved.

Reading about the ancient Israelites leaves me perplexed as to how they could've *repeatedly* been so forgetful of God. Among much else, He gave them the plagues, the parting of the Red Sea, and the law at Sinai, and they *still* managed to distance themselves from Him, preferring their own way. I wonder the same about Jesus' closest friends. They ate, slept, and breathed with Him for three years straight, but when His story took an unexpected turn—toward death—they resumed life as normal as if the whole relationship were unfounded (see John 21:3; Mark 16:11). And then I wonder about me. I'm like a broken record of asking, waiting, and seeing Him come through, at which point I trust. But then, at some point, I forget to ask or forget that He always comes through or forget about Him, period, and walk aimlessly in disbelief—until I remember again. So I guess I'm really dense, too, or just a girl who needs to be reminded of her Savior.

My friend Jake died of a brain tumor in 2005. I remember a few months before his death praying in his living room and asking what he wanted. When he didn't mention healing, I was a bit perplexed. "The thing is, Abbie, I know I'm fallible right now. I'm well aware that at any moment I could die, making me similarly aware of every breath's gift. If God heals me, I know normality will return and I'll be unloosed from such gratitude and ceaseless dependence. I know I'll forget how it feels to need God, whereas right now, every cell of my existence is awakened to its need for God. And I don't want healing from that."

Through history, humans have benefited from modes of binding the Law to our bodies in order to remember. Scripture offers some interesting examples here, too, such as tassels and bodily markings. Our day and age seems to like jewelry, clothing, and tattoos bearing aspects of Christ, yet, in all of these, it's important to remember that they are not our end. Life—all of life, including the sexual, partial, painful grounds—is a training ground for eternity and our participation in an eternally redeemed creation. It's a ground of preparation, remembering what is passed, hoping toward the wedding feast to come, and fulfilling vows between God and His radiant bride, the church.

Rules are not all bad, but they do have the potential to put us on a deadly treadmill. If not handled with fragility, rules rope us into rituals and mock us with morality and guilt. I dated a guy who had index cards taped all over his dashboard. They spoke of good character and living for Jesus instead of lust and the world. I thought they were weird and an odd form of brainwashing (but apparently not *that* weird, because I kept dating him). Plus, never once did I hear him refer to them or reference their effect on his existence. It was as though by taping them to his line of vision, he assumed they would automatically tape themselves to his heart as he drove down the freeway. But that's not how biblical meditation works. Allowing God's thoughts to become a part of mine and my memory is wise and, I believe, transformative. Expecting magical transformations from Scotch tape or semantic regurgitations is not. Knowing God's thoughts is an essential part of knowing Him, but we must treat our humanity with more dignity than putting our hopes in the likes of magic tricks. Renowned psychologist and spiritual director David Benner said,

> Discipline, spiritual or otherwise, is a good servant, but a bad master. It is not the summum bonum — the supreme good. When it is valued in and of itself, the disciplined life easily leads to rigidity and pride. . . . Jesus showed nothing of this rigidity. Although the strength of his resolve and consistency of his spiritual disciplines are striking, he lived a life characterized by flexibility, not predictability. He was constantly surprising people — always capable of spontaneously embracing the opportunities of the moment, never compulsively grasping the safety of the habitual. His discipline served to align his will and his spirit with God's will and God's Spirit. But this discipline was not dependent on external rigidity. It sprang from a heart that was aflame with the love of God, not a will that was striving for self-control. Pride and rigidity are the chain-mail armor we use to protect ourselves from vulnerability.[1]

My friend Ashley is young to interactions with Jesus. She grew up around the church but kept herself abstinent from its ways and attention. Recently, she came to me saying she wanted a promise ring (communicating one's choice to abstain from sex before marriage): "I want my life to be pure from here on out. I want to believe what you told me about God being able to pick up the pieces from my raunchy path." I'm usually not keen on such products of our evangelical subculture but was encouraged by her desire to explore the potential of this accessory.

Ashley grew up in and out of the projects and has been in

Hollywood ever since. Her past is extremely sexual, and she has run with porn and trafficking circles since she was twelve. Add drugs to her equation and you've got a girl who has lived in hell for much of her two-decade time on earth. Yet Jesus found a way into her heart and she's fallen quite hard for this new and foreign lover. Public confessions or personalized mementos of remembrance, like a promise ring, can sometimes act as significant reminders that we have, in fact, been saved by God's grace and are prone to forget our true identities. For Ashley, this ring represents new birth, and although its promise is still up for grabs, every time she looks at her hand, she gives God another chance to remind her of her new identity in Christ.

Ashley's purity will be compromised again, not because she's a sinner by choice, but because she's a sinner by nature. And she's also a saint, meaning that purity will always be a part of her, even when impurity visits (see Titus 1:15). In Christ, we are both sinner and saint, which should be encouraging for the soul who's slept with seventy-seven people and for the one who's been chaste her whole life. To know our purity is to know we are made in the image of God, and to know our impurity is to know our image of God is marred. There's no place we've gone, in mind or in action, that disqualifies us from Christ's purity or the partaking of His clean slate. Nothing of our past is beyond divine repair (see Psalm 103:12).

It may sound too simplistic or cliché, but Jesus is, in fact, our only proper answer to any of these conversations. Only He has lived the wholly human life, dependent, submissive, and alive in His Father. Only He has known lust apart from sin and life in its most purposed state of being sexual, whole, and holy. And only He has the capacity and creativity to reorient and order our sexuality and humanity in such a way that we might live resurrected and loved through the life of the Resurrection and Love Himself.

We find deepest life when we're found in the Life of Another. And when we're found in the Life of Another, our stories become better, more meaningful and lively. Our stories of singleness, sexuality, longing, home, desperation, identity, beauty, and sorrow find life when enraptured by the life and story of God. *I* am most me when I am found in God. And God is found most in me when I find myself in Him—when I abide—waiting, watching, and believing by faith that He is good and at work in my every need (see Philippians 4:19). Handicaps haunt me at times, and thorns prevail in my flesh, but the glorifying will of God remains. My truest Lover is a Person with a face and a ferocious persistence toward my depths. And my story as a single comes alive when I choose to live loved in the story of God.

FOR FURTHER MUSING AND DISCUSSION

1. The following quote differentiates Christianity from any other world religion:

> If my basis for right standing with God involves following a rule, I will eventually fall short. But if my basis centers around the undefinable shape of a *Person* named Love, the pressure is off. I no longer have to look perfect, have all the answers, or be in control, because *He is*. Mere religion forms moral people who hope they're loved; Christ forms human beings who know they're loved.

   What's freeing to you about following this God of the Bible? What areas do you wrestle to believe or live out on a day-to-day basis?

2. It's tempting to think that sexuality is about lusts and that lusts are about hormonally charged single Christians who have no healthy outlet. But that's not true. Sexuality—including lusts, longings, beauty, and emotion—is privy to the married and to the single alike. Discovering our sexuality lasts a lifetime, as does discovering what it means to follow Jesus. What's difficult to believe about this? What's liberating?

"Real isn't how you are made," said the Skin Horse. "It's a thing that happens to you. . . ."

"Does it happen all at once, like being wound up," he asked, "or bit by bit?"

"It doesn't happen all at once," said the Skin Horse. "You become. It takes a long time. That's why it doesn't happen often to people who break easily, or have sharp edges, or who have to be carefully kept. Generally, by the time you are Real, most of your hair has been loved off, and your eyes drop out and you get loose in your joints and very shabby. But these things don't matter at all, because once you are Real you can't be ugly, except to people who don't understand."

MARGERY WILLIAMS, *The Velveteen Rabbit*

CHAPTER 18

SINGLE UNION

My beloved speaks and says to me: "Arise, my love, my beautiful one, and come away, for behold, the winter is past; the rain is over and gone."

SONG OF SOLOMON 2:10-11

Love is therefore the fundamental and innate vocation of every human being.

POPE JOHN PAUL II

That they may all be one, just as you, Father, are in me, and I in you, that they also may be in us, so that the world may believe that you have sent me. The glory that you have given me I have given to them, that they may be one even as we are one, I in them and you in me, that they may become perfectly one, so that the world may know that you sent me and loved them even as you loved me. Father, I desire that they also, whom you have given me, may be with me where I am, to see my glory that you have given me because you loved me before the foundation of the world.

JOHN 17:21-24

I WAKE TO an Enemy who thwarts truth and shatters good, and Another who makes every effort to clarify Truth and rescue what is good. One blurs hope and binds my living, while the other brings me new vision to see the creation and myself alive. The Judas in me wants my own way. And the I in me keeps searching for answers and conclusive end points. But I'm recognizing that the areas of my life I most rigorously try to protect are similarly those that are most scared of being loved. I'm remembering and realizing anew that following God is less about perfection, or perfect understanding, and more about learning to trust Jesus. My single covenant is more about choosing Love than knowing Love's answer.

We start and end with union. Embryos start when an egg and a sperm unite. And death unites us with either dust or absolute communion. And since the beginning, God has been telling a story of creation, love, and restoration based not on a sparkly diamond but on professed faith in Jesus Christ and what it is He did in stepping out of heaven and bearing the weight of our fall upon His shoulders, paving the way for reestablished union with the Love story for which we were made.

The book of Revelation is filled with Eden imagery, and the book of Genesis with marital imagery. The cry of both is restoration. God's final chapters reveal thoughts on the future marriage. In that day, our union together will be (re)established as it was in the beginning and will remain forevermore—a restored earth and creation, with no crying or pain (see Revelation 21:4), no confusion about our true Home (see 2 Corinthians 5:1-8). The chase toward Home is at the heart of every human being. But beneath that, in the very bowels of the soul, there's an even deeper desire to be chased, loved, and caught—welcomed into an eternal union.

As singles pursuing Jesus as our center, we've been given a unique path toward expressing the wholeness of masculinity and femininity and profoundly mysterious (see Ephesians 5:32) complements herein. We are designed to function in union—intimate, committed, covenantal union. As explored throughout these pages, both marrieds and singles have a divinely created wiring for exclusive and lifelong commitment and intimacy, modeled by the experience of community in the Trinity. Marriage enables this within the relationship of God and spouse, while singleness does so with God, the church, and non-exclusive bonds of friendship.

Though many of us will get married, marriage is not a promise of God nor a prerequisite to our maturity or spiritual capacity.

God promises that He will be with us, He is enough for us, and He is our ultimate Bridegroom (see Matthew 22:1-14; Luke 20:35; Revelation 19), meaning there is an end to singleness. There is a day coming when we, the children of God, will be at the wedding feast of the Lamb and will be His bride. And though many of us will receive the gift of marriage on this side of heaven, that will never be our ultimate end or union. Earthly marriage and earthly singleness both have their conclusion in death, acting as but a hint of what is to come in our spiritual union and eternal marriage.

Our invitation—in both singleness and marriage, weakness and strength, desires and desperations, dreams and frustrations, sexuality and beauty, solitude and community—is union with God now and forevermore. We were made for the story of God, and we are fundamentally incomplete in and of our own. We are made to find God as our refuge in life's chasms—already but not yet, free but bound, saved but still falling—because of His story. Although completely unique, we are fully enmeshed, entangled in His grace. Although fully in process, we've been fully written into His story, and His story into ours. My greatest task, then, my primary rule and lifelong vocation, is but waking to the Author, awakening to the Romance, waiting well toward the eternal Wedding.

Following ten steps or losing ten pounds won't find you a husband or fix your insecurity, and busyness or bitterness toward those you dated or those who never asked you out won't heal your heart's brokenness. For whatever divine reasons, where you are is where God has you—on purpose, for His purposes and your ultimate good. God hasn't forgotten you or your desires or failed to hear your requests. The life of the Trinity is authoring your story, and only through expressions of His will will you find fulfillments of yours—of unity and sexuality, holiness and chastity, and abundant life in your sainthood and humanity.

FOR FURTHER MUSING AND DISCUSSION

1. This is the crux of these pages:

> We were designed to function in union—intimate, committed, covenantal union. As explored throughout these pages, both marrieds and singles have a divinely created wiring for exclusive and lifelong commitment and intimacy, modeled by the experience of community in the Trinity. Marriage enables this within the relationship of God and spouse, while singleness does so with God, the church, and non-exclusive bonds of friendship.

What aspects of singleness do you understand better after reading this far? What aspects are you still interested in exploring further?

2. Consider Revelation 21:1-4:

> Then I saw a new heaven and a new earth, for the first heaven and the first earth had passed away, and the sea was no more. And I saw the holy city, new Jerusalem, coming down out of heaven from God, prepared as a bride adorned for her husband. And I heard a loud voice from the throne saying, "Behold, the dwelling place of God is with man. He will dwell with them, and they will be his people, and God himself will be with them as their God. He will wipe away every tear from their eyes, and death shall be no more, neither shall there be mourning, nor crying, nor pain anymore, for the former things have passed away."

What might this have to do with sexuality? Describe your idea of a "redeemed sexuality" (as it will be in the restored creation).

Once there was God,
who breathed life to earth and earth to life.
He drew a sky and colored a sun,
lighting the image of one called man.
From man He drew woman
and called this drawing good.

Brushes were given to all,
And free reign to tasting all colors but one.
And that one became all that was wanted.
God knew of such lusts, however,
and the costs a free canvas would incur,
and He let the painting go on.
He stroked a way for freedom
and staked a way for freedom's fall.

At one point, He drew me.
He addressed that I'd get lost
and assured that I had a Way Home.
"My sight could never lose you;
from My body you cannot be removed."
He asked if I'd be part of His story
and proposed that I make Him part of mine.
I said, "Yes."
"From this day forward,
till death do us fully unite,
I am Yours and You are mine.
You are my story,
my single story."

I still wrestle, though,
wondering if He really knows
the complexity of my colors
and inconsistency of my ways?
He says He does and that He still wants to be with me,
that I am still worth His yes.
"You are essential in My painting.
Your every part imagined before time,
every single part.
From this day forward, till death do us fully unite,
I am yours and you are Mine.
You are My story,
My single story."

EPILOGUE OF A MRS.

IT'S BEEN FOUR years since I started scribing the contents of *Celibate Sex*. Somewhere in the latter half of this, I sat next to a man in church named Micah. We fell in love, pretty much that morning, and married nine months later.

Even though much has changed because I am married, much has stayed the same. I'm still learning about sexuality and what it means to be a woman and feminine. I'm still learning about love and what it means to be chaste. I'm still learning what it means to wait *well* and proactively, which may be one of the hardest postures on this side of the new creation. I'm still learning about submission to the created order and the beauty this offers. I'm still learning about dating and answering genuinely, with Truth and Spirit, the questions of singles. I still have unmet hopes and dreams and desires. I still get lonely and struggle with insecurity more than I like to admit, even when my best friend is lying next to me. And I'm still learning what it means to follow Jesus.

As to whether I'd change anything about these pages post-altar or have experienced a change of beliefs since they've been written, I wouldn't, and I really haven't. At times, in fact, I still find myself retreating to conversations and consolations learned in singleness, as I realize it was such a spacious time of self- and God-discovery. I'm still wanting to grow in disciplines such as letting go of expectations too often put on my husband to be my ultimate union and communion. I try to remember that Micah and I are a temporary pair when it comes to eternity. And that ultimately we are God's and made to live out *God's* story, one of love and abundant life, designed to sanctify us in holiness and prepare us to face our Savior with the familiar, disarming tones of "I know you and you know Me."

Most marrieds will tell you that many of the problems they face now are no different than those they encountered as singles but, for whatever reason, ignored. And now they're watching those issues resurface with greater complexity and sometimes be directed at their spouse. That said, no matter where your story leads you in days ahead, this season is not in vain. If you are single, God is sanctifying you toward holiness and you have an important and unique role in the Body of Christ. If you marry one day, God will continue this undertaking, drawing you toward Himself and toward becoming your true self. All of life is a training ground toward the life to come—eternal life in a restored creation, eternal union and communion with God and the communion of saints. May we live it alive, with gratitude, knowing that He is at work in all things and that in all things, we are His thoughtful workmanship, bought at a price and born for a Story more wonderful than we can imagine.

DTR: DEFINING THE RHETORIC[1]

celibate: 1. a person who abstains from sexual relations. 2. a person who remains unmarried, esp. for religious reasons. 3. observing or pertaining to sexual abstention or a religious vow not to marry. 4. not married.

chastity: "Purposefully turning away for a time from dwelling upon or engaging in the sexual dimension of our relationship to others—even our husband or wife—and thus learning how not to be governed by this powerful aspect of our life."

Christian: 2. of, pertaining to, believing in, or belonging to the religion based on the teachings of Christ.

church: 3. *(sometimes initial capital letter)* the whole body of Christian believers; Christendom.

date: 7. a social appointment, engagement, or occasion arranged beforehand with another person.

human sexuality: how people experience the erotic and express themselves as sexual beings. Frequently driven by the desire for sexual pleasure, human sexuality has biological, physical, and emotional aspects. Biologically, it refers to the reproductive mechanism as well as the basic biological drive that exists in all species and can encompass sexual intercourse and sexual contact in all its forms. Emotional aspects deal with the intense emotions relating to sexual acts and associated social bonds. Physical issues around sexuality range from purely medical considerations to concerns about the physiological or even psychological and sociological aspects of sexual behavior. The term can also cover cultural, political, legal, and philosophical aspects. It may also refer to issues of morality, ethics, theology, spirituality, or religion and how they relate to all things sexual.

married: 4. interconnected or joined; united.

nuclear family: a term developed in the western world to distinguish the family group consisting of parents, most commonly father and mother, and their children, from what is known as extended family.

seduction: 1. the act of persuading somebody to do something wrong. 2. the act of persuading somebody to have sex, especially by using a romantic or deceptive approach. 3. something that tempts, persuades, or attracts.

sex: 2. the sum of the structural and functional differences by which the male and female are distinguished, or the phenomena or behavior dependent on these differences. 3. the instinct or attraction drawing one sex toward another, or its manifestation in life and conduct. 8. to have sex, to engage in sexual intercourse.

single: 5. pertaining to the unmarried state: the single life.

singleness: the state or quality of being single.

Trinity: the union of three persons of the Christian God, the Father, Jesus Christ, the Son, and the Holy Spirit, in a single Godhead.

union: 1. the act of joining together people or things to form a whole.

NOTES

INTRODUCTION

1. See *The Slow Fade* (Colorado Springs, CO: David C. Cook, 2010), a book I wrote with Reggie Joiner and Chuck Bomar about people age eighteen to thirty-five fading from the church. Much of this fade relates to single people being unsure of their status as unmarried and therefore unable to securely assimilate into adulthood.

CHAPTER 1: FIG LEAVES

1. I am a feminist to the degree that I believe in women and believe that women deserve rights, justice, and fairness of treatment. And I'm more than willing to fight for the fullest measure of strength, beauty, and holistic empowerment for both men and women. I am not a feminist, however, to the degree that I believe that women and men are the same. I believe we are different, from physical and emotional makeup to physiological and sociological behavior. And I believe we are equally valuable in God's eyes—like apples and oranges—uniquely designed for different roles and responsibilities.
2. Henri J. M. Nouwen, *The Road to Daybreak* (New York: Image, 1990), 144–145.
3. Also known as Satan, the Enemy, or the Devil.

CHAPTER 2: SEX AND UNION

1. Paul K. Jewett, *Man as Male and Female* (Grand Rapids, MI: Eerdmans, 1990), 172.
2. Eugene H. Peterson, *Reversed Thunder* (New York: HarperOne, 1991), 147.
3. For more here, consider Stanley Grenz, *Sexual Ethics: A Biblical Perspective* (Dallas: Word, 1990), 31–37.
4. John W. De Gruchy, *Dietrich Bonhoeffer: Witness to Jesus Christ* (Minneapolis: Augsburg Fortress, 1991), 60.
5. Holiness is initially God's nature, not ours. Therefore, our being holy is our being in relationship—union—with the God who is holy.

CHAPTER 3: ALONE

1. *La Vie en Rose* (Legende Films, 2007).
2. See John 4:7-26 (Jesus reaching out to the woman at the well); 11:17-27 (turning to Mary and Martha upon Lazarus's death); 13:23 (the disciple Jesus loved).

CHAPTER 4: BODILY SPEAKING

1. Ray S. Anderson and Dennis B. Guernsey, *On Being Family* (Grand Rapids, MI: Eerdmans, 1985), 156.
2. Susan Annette Muto, *Celebrating the Single Life: A Spirituality for Single Persons in Today's World* (Bombay, India: St. Paul's, 1995), 188.

CHAPTER 5: SPIRITUAL ORGASMS

1. Luke 19:41; John 11:35.
2. Leviticus 11:44; 1 Peter 1:16.
3. Matthew 14:13; 15:39; 26:36-44.
4. Luke 15.
5. A particularly helpful resource for this is Merle Jordan's *Reclaiming Your Story* (Louisville, KY: Westminster John Knox, 1999).

CHAPTER 6: DATING

1. Chap Clark has written extensively on modern teens. See *Hurt: Inside the World of Today's Teenagers* (Ada, MI: Baker, 2005). David Kinnaman has as well. See *unChristian: What a New Generation Really Thinks About Christianity . . . and Why It Matters* (Baker, 2007) and *You Lost Me: Why Young Christians Are Leaving Church . . . and Rethinking Faith* (Baker, 2011).
2. See Acts 5:1-10.

CHAPTER 8: SUBMISSION AND BEAUTY

1. Various challenges today make this biblical precept difficult, such as divorce, fatherless families, and negligence in churches toward singles. Depending on the context, then, it may be up to a single woman to seek out such a man, group of men, or couple whom she respects and values as a significant voice in her life and whom she'd feel safe coming "under the wings of."
2. What about the fall of man and its corruptions of beauty? It's tough to pinpoint how the physical sides of beauty were affected by the Fall, but it's fair to say that all sides of beauty (body, soul, mind, and spirit, among others) were rescued by the death of Christ on the cross and His subsequent rising. Thus, justified beauty is in our midst, as are portions still being sanctified. To have eyes to recognize both may be a lovely prayer.
3. "Beatific vision," Wikipedia, http://en.wikipedia.org/wiki/Beatific_vision.

CHAPTER 9: INVOLUNTARY SINGLENESS

1. "America's Families and Living Arrangements: 2010," *United States Census Bureau*, http://www.census.gov/population/www/socdemo/hh-fam/cps2010.html.
2. Richard Foster, *Freedom of Simplicity* (New York: HarperOne, 2005), 172, 76.
3. Miguel A. De La Torre, *A Lily Among the Thorns: Imagining a*

New Christian Sexuality (San Francisco: Jossey-Bass, 2007), 54.

4. Saint Augustine, *The Literal Meaning of Genesis*, vol. 1 (Long Prairie, MN: Newman Press, 1982), IX:7–12.

5. J. Pelikan and H. T. Lehmann, eds., *Luther's Works*, 55 vols. (Philadelphia: Fortress; St. Louis: Concordia, 1955), 49:142.

6. See Stanley J. Grenz, *The Social God and the Relational Self* (Louisville, KY: Westminster John Knox, 2001) for a more robust undertaking here.

CHAPTER 10: SACRED DIMENSIONS OF WAITING

1. God never addresses "the one" I'm supposed to marry. Rather, He seems to center on *how* I choose to love, in giving and in receiving. His aim is about getting *to me*, and if that's through a who (man, woman, friend), where (location), or when (timing), He'll lead accordingly. Likewise, God isn't out to get me or trap me but rather to woo me and convince me that I'm loved.

2. Matthew Lee Anderson, *Earthen Vessels: Why Our Bodies Matter to Our Faith* (Ada, MI: Bethany, 2011), 27.

3. Anderson, 31.

4. Henri J. M. Nouwen, *In the Name of Jesus: Reflections on Christian Leadership* (Danvers, MA: Crossroad Publishing, 1992), 77.

5. Dallas Willard, *Renovation of the Heart* (Colorado Springs, CO: NavPress, 2002), 170–171, 94.

CHAPTER 11: BROKENNESS AND LUST

1. This poem was written for a friend I've grown to love.

2. Jean Vanier, *Community and Growth*, rev. ed. (Mahwah, NJ, Paulist, 1989), 265.

3. Vanier, 280.

4. A thoughtful work on this subject is Marnie C. Ferree, *No Stones: Women Redeemed from Sexual Addiction*, 2nd ed. (Downers

Grove, IL: InterVarsity, 2010).

5. Larry Crabb, *Connecting* (Nashville: Thomas Nelson, 2004), 66.

6. I can't remember who said it, but I do remember that the speaker based it on 1 John 1.

CHAPTER 12: SEX

1. Matthew Schmitz, "Premarital Sex in America," *The Witherspoon Institute*, March 4, 2011, http://www.thepublicdiscourse.com/2011/03/2871.

2. "Six Reasons Young Christians Leave Church," *Barna Group*, September 28, 2011, http://www.barna.org/teens-next -gen-articles/528-six-reasons-young-christians-leave -church?q=sex.

3. Dallas Willard, *Renovation of the Heart* (Colorado Springs, CO: NavPress, 2002), 159–160.

4. Judith K. and Jack O. Balswick, *Authentic Human Sexuality: An Integrated Christian Approach* (Downers Grove, IL: InterVarsity, 2008), 14–15, 63.

5. Mary Stewart Van Leeuwen, in Balswick, 71.

CHAPTER 13: BOUNDARIES

1. Susan Annette Muto, *Celebrating the Single Life: A Spirituality for Single Persons in Today's World* (Bombay, India: St. Paul's, 1995), 121.

2. Muto, 148, 155.

3. Ubuntu is a humanist philosophy focusing on people's allegiances and relations with each other. The word has its origin in the Bantu languages of southern Africa and is seen as a traditional African concept.

4. "Desmond Tutu's Recipe for Peace," http://www.beliefnet.com/Inspiration/2004/04/Desmond-Tutus-Recipe-For-Peace.aspx?p=2.

5. Ask yourself in this case what happens when "just a friend" starts dating someone. It's usually pretty telling.

6. See Amnon's hatred for Tamar (whom he'd raped) in 2 Samuel 13:15.
7. Margot Starbuck, *Unsqueezed* (Downers Grove, IL: InterVarsity, 2010), 139.
8. More suitable translations here seem to be the NASB, "Watch over your heart with all diligence, for from it flow the springs of life," and the ESV, "Keep your heart with all vigilance, for from it flow the springs of life."
9. The BOUNDARIES books, by Henry Cloud and John Townsend, are practical resources that explore this topic more fully.
10. Matthew Henry, *An Exposition of the Old and New Testament* (New York: Robert Carter and Brothers, 1856), commentary on Proverbs 4.

CHAPTER 14: GUILTY AND FORGIVEN

1. Phyllis Tickle, *The Divine Hours: Prayers for Summertime* (New York: Doubleday, 2000).
2. Read Romans 7 for a fuller picture here.
3. A. W. Tozer, *The Knowledge of the Holy* (New York: HarperCollins, 1961), 1.

CHAPTER 15: MASTURBATION AND CHASTITY

1. Richard Dobbins, PhD, *Teaching Your Children the Truth About Sex* (Lake Mary, FL: Siloam Press, 2006).
2. Dr. James Dobson, *Breakaway Magazine*, Focus on the Family, July 2002.
3. Lauren F. Winner, "Sex in the Body of Christ," *Christianity Today*, May 2005, vol. 45, no. 5.
4. Lauren F. Winner, *Real Sex* (Grand Rapids, MI: Baker, 2006), 128–129.
5. *The Renovaré Spiritual Formation Bible,* New Revised Standard Version (New York: Harper Collins, 1989), 2296.

6. C. S. Lewis, *Mere Christianity* (New York: Harper Collins, 2001), 101–102.

CHAPTER 16: WAITING WELL

1. See David G. Benner, *The Gift of Being Yourself* (Downers Grove, IL: InterVarsity, 2004).
2. Rarely does someone smoke because it's cool or tastes good; they do so because they've found a behavior that speaks into their felt need (stress, angst, fatigue).
3. A theme and theology scattered throughout the Scriptures, with John 18 being one exposition of this.
4. Edith Schaeffer, *Hidden Art* (Carol Stream, IL: Tyndale, 1971), 40.
5. Again, Edith Schaeffer's *Hidden Art* (or later editions were titled *The Hidden Art of Homemaking*) is a thoughtful book that indirectly addresses such topics for singles.

CHAPTER 17: LOVE'S RULE

1. David G. Benner, *Desiring God's Will* (Downers Grove, IL: InterVarsity, 2005), 25.

DTR: DEFINING THE RHETORIC

1. Definitions are drawn from www.dictionary.com, with the exception of "chastity," which comes from *The Renovaré Spiritual Formation Bible*, and "human sexuality" and "nuclear family," which come from www.wikipedia.org.

ABOUT THE AUTHOR

ABBIE SMITH resides in Savannah, Georgia, with her husband, Micah, and their daughter, Elliana. Although roles as a wife and new mom keep her busy, she continues to write and speak as her schedule permits. On a given day, Abbie may be found counseling girls at a local coffee shop, tutoring kids in her inner-city neighborhood, or writing college-age mentoring material (www.xp3college.org). She has a bachelor's degree in religious studies from Emory University and a master's degree in spiritual formation and soul care from Talbot University. Visit her at www.unsteadysaint.com.

More powerful books on issues for women from NavPress.

Beautiful Battlefields
Bo Stern

How do you gain the strength to fight continual life battles with faith, courage, and security, all while being assured that you aren't alone? Bo Stern offers a hopeful message on pain that goes to the center of the gospel: God's promise to fight with us and never leave us alone.

978-1-61291-319-3

Every Thought Captive
Jerusha Clark

Every Thought Captive explores the unique nature of the female mind and examines the sources of our fears and anxieties. Drawing from personal experiences, including struggles with anorexia and depression, best-selling author Jerusha Clark shares the freedom found in shifting our thoughts from the everyday to the eternal.

978-1-57683-868-6

The Life You Crave
Jerusha Clark

Everyone desires God's best for her life, but in a world of ever-expanding options and lots of advice, what is the best way to pursue a life well lived? Author Jerusha Clark believes that God has given us the gift of discernment, which will lead us to what is truly His best.

978-1-60006-055-7

To order copies, call NavPress at **1-800-366-7788** or log on to **www.NavPress.com**.

The Message Means Understanding

Bringing the Bible to all ages

*T*he Message is written in contemporary language that is much like talking with a good friend. When paired with your favorite Bible study, The Message will deliver a reading experience that is reliable, energetic, and amazingly fresh.

NAVESSENTIALS

Voices of The Navigators—Past, Present, and Future

NAVESSENTIALS offer core Navigator messages from Jim Downing, LeRoy Eims, Mike Treneer, and others — at an affordable price. This series will deeply influence generations in the movement of discipleship. Learn from the old and new messages of The Navigators how powerful and transformational the life of a disciple truly is.

The Triumph of Surrender
by William M. Fletcher
9781615219070 | $5.00

Meditation
by Jim Downing
9781615217250 | $5.00

Advancing the Gospel
by Mike Treneer
9781617471575 | $5.00

Laboring in the Harvest
by LeRoy Eims with Randy Eims
9781615216406 | $10.99

To order, go to **NavPress.com** or call **1-800-366-7788**.

Facebook.com/NavPressPublishing   Twitter.com/NavPress

NAVPRESS
Discipleship Inside Out*

Support the Ministry of The Navigators

The Navigators' calling is to advance the gospel of Jesus and His kingdom into the nations through spiritual generations of laborers living and discipling among the lost.

Navigators have invested their lives in people for more than 75 years, coming alongside them life on life to help them passionately know Christ and to make Him known.

The U.S. Navigators' ministry touches lives in varied settings, including college campuses, military bases, downtown offices, urban neighborhoods, prisons, and youth camps.

Dedicated to helping people navigate spiritually, The Navigators aims to make a permanent difference in the lives of people around the world. The Navigators helps its communities of friends to follow Christ passionately and equip them effectively to go out and do the same.

To learn more about donating to The Navigators' ministry,
go to **www.navigators.org/us/support**
or call toll-free at **1-866-568-7827**.